BASIC AND ADVANCED
LIGHT PLANE MAINTENANCE

EGT Systems

The Light Plane Maintenance Library
Volume Seven

BASIC AND ADVANCED
LIGHT PLANE MAINTENANCE

EGT Systems

By Kas Thomas and
the Editors of *Light Plane*
Maintenance Magazine

Belvoir Publications Inc.
Greenwich, Connecticut 06836

ISBN: 0-9613139-8-6

Please Note: The information appearing in this publication is presented for educational purposes only. In no case shall the publishers be held responsible for any use readers may choose to make (or not to make) of this information. Readers are hereby advised that Federal Aviation Regulation 91.163(a) places primary responsibility for ensuring the airworthy condition of any aircraft on the aircraft owner or operator. Any person who performs inspections, alterations, and/or repairs on any aircraft does so entirely at his or her own risk.

Contents

Preface   **vi**

Introduction   **1**
    Why Monitor Exhaust Gas Temperature?
    How Is EGT Measured?
    What About Cylinder Head Temperature?
    EGT: The Key to Understanding Your Engine

Chapter 1:   Internal Combustion Fundamentals   **13**
    The Otto Cycle
    Ignition
    Fuel & Air
    The Compression Stroke
    Turbocharging

Chapter 2:   Principles of Mixture Management   **33**
    The Effect of Fuel/Air Ratio on EGT
    Mixture Maldistribution
    Material Limitations
    Special Considerations for Turbocharged Engines
    Mixture Management by Phase of Flight

Chapter 3:   Cruise-Leaning Setpoints   **59**
    Best-Power Mixture
    Peak EGT
    Best-Economy Mixture

Chapter 4:   Cylinder Head Temperature (CHT)   **69**
    Shock Cooling
    Overheating
    Troubleshooting with CHT

Chapter 5:   Abnormal Combustion   **81**
    Tetraethyl Lead
    Rich vs. Lean Octane Ratings
    Octane Anomalies
    Detonation's Mode of Action
    Factors Affecting Detonation

Chapter 6: Troubleshooting with EGT   **99**
What Does an EGT Probe Measure?
Timing Effects
Magneto Failure
Spark Plug Fouling
Induction System Anomalies
Loss of Compression
Detonation & Preignition
Fuel Contamination

Chapter 7: EGT Installation Guidelines   **115**
Installing EGT Probes
Cockpit Display Installation
CHT Probes
GEM Installation Tips

Chapter 8: EGT Ergonomics   **129**
Switchable Multichannel Systems
Digital vs. Analog Display
Scanning Devices
All-Cylinder Displays: Analog
All-Cylinder Displays: Digital

APPENDICES

Appendix A: Manufacturers   **144**
Appendix B: The Graphic Engine Monitor   **145**
        In Operation
Basic Modes of Action
Using the GEM on the Ground
Using the GEM on Takeoff
Leaning the Engine in Flight

Glossary   **153**

Index   **163**

Preface

The aviation world has long needed a book on exhaust gas temperature (EGT) systems. Not only has mixture management become more complicated over the years—with the increased use of turbochargers, fuel injection, etc.—but *EGT systems themselves* have become more complex, what with a variety of multiprobe, digital, automatic scanning, switchable, and other types of systems having come into widespread acceptance in the past ten years. Oddly, very few EGT systems get installed in brand-new airplanes. (To this day, factory installations remain primarily single-probe systems, wired to just one exhaust stack.) Most installations have been done as retrofits, which means that most pilots have gotten no formal instruction in how to use their EGT equipment. (Probably just as well, since Certified Flight Instructors generally aren't experts on EGT/TIT interpretation.)

Exhaust gas temperature gauges were, of course, originally touted as aids for leaning. (Cessna for years called its optional-equipment EGT systems "economy mixture indicators.") The sophisticated owner-operator knows, however, that an EGT system is far more than a mere leaning tool. In fact, intelligent mixture management is really only a side-benefit of EGT ownership. The true value of EGT lies in the opportunity it gives the pilot to *see inside the combustion process*. The unusual diagnostic capabilities of the EGT make it a powerful troubleshooting tool, allowing the technically adept owner to understand far more about his or her engine than "which cylinder is leanest" or "which cylinder is hottest."

No less formidable than the diagnostic potential of the EGT/TIT gauge is the level of technical understanding of the combustion process needed to use it intelligently. Interpretation of EGT data is often difficult, unless the user fully understands all ramifications of the combustion process. And the latter is an area fraught, as Pogo might say, with subtitles.

Alcor, Electronics International, Insight Instrument Corp., J.P. Instruments, and K.S. Avionics all have published useful technical literature on the operation of their products, but to date no single book-length manual exists that discusses the operation, installation, and interpretation of *all* major types of EGTs. The purpose of this book

Research for this book went far beyond the manufacturers' literature. Many hours were spent searching through service bulletins and technical papers, talking to experts in the field (including Al Hundere, widely regarded as the father of the modern EGT), and culling critical findings from such industry standards as C.F. Taylor's *The Internal Combustion Engine in Theory and Practice* (MIT Press, 1985), Colin Ferguson's *Internal Combustion Engines: Applied Thermodynamics* (Wiley, 1986), and John B. Heywood's magnificent *Internal Combustion Engine Fundamentals* (McGraw-Hill, 1988). Also, in the process of writing this book, I had the opportunity to participate in the installation of a full-pop GEM 603 system on a turbocharged Lycoming IO-360; I had the opportunity to fly (not just for an hour or two, but for periods of up to 35 and 40 hours each) all of the major types of EGTs in current use; and I had the chance to actually troubleshoot some developing engine problems in a Piper Seminole (ignition-related, as it turned out) via EGT.

Like the other books in the *LPM Library* series, the present volume attempts to broaden the pilot's understanding of his or her airplane, not only in terms of how the systems work and interact, but how the *pilot* interacts with those systems to make the *entire* system—the airplane as a whole—last longer and (we hope) function more reliably. In this regard, *EGT Systems* dovetails with concepts presented in *Top End* (and foreshadows material in later volumes—*Maintaining Power* in particular). For the benefit of the raw beginner—and to enhance the value of *EGT Systems* in its own right—a review of the Otto cycle is included in Chapter One; however, if terms like "valve guide," "camshaft," or "exhaust manifold" are unfamiliar to you, you'll want to refer to *Top End* as necessary.

Much of what I know about exhaust analysis comes from conversations over a period of years with Al Hundere of Alcor, Inc. and John Youngquist (founder of Insight Instrument Corp. and designer of the Graphic Engine Monitor). Every plane owner owes a debt of gratitude to both of these men, without whose efforts the state of the EGT art would be nowhere near where it is today. I have benefitted, also, from conversations with Bill Simpkinson of K.S. Avionics, whose products have often shown remarkable innovation and always reflect a caring attitude toward plane-owners. Helpful as these experts have been, any errors of fact or interpretation appearing in this book (and there are bound to be one or two, despite my best efforts) should be credited to the author's account, and no one else's.

Very special thanks go to my wife, Rita, for putting up with the disruptions to daily life that inevitably result from a book project. Also, I wish to acknowledge the help of Belvoir Publications (David Shugarts, in particular) in getting this book to a state of fruition. Last but not least, I wish to thank my readers for making this project (as any junior MBA would say) *viable*.

May your engine go 500 hours beyond TBO.

Kas Thomas
Greenwich, CT
September 12, 1988

Introduction

Exhaust gas temperature (EGT) instrumentation has been around for so long now, and is so well accepted, that it is easy to forget how that technology came about in the first place. The historical record is a bit unclear as to whether Al Hundere or Ed Swearingen first "invented" the EGT, although it should be remembered that turbine inlet and outlet temperature (TIT and TOT) systems had already been developed for jet engines in the 1950s, and the science of thermocouple pyrometry was well advanced even before then. The question is really one of who was first to adapt the jet-engine TIT/TOT indicator (using K-type thermocouple probes) to piston-engine use, and why.

Al Hundere, founder of Alcor, Inc., modestly admits that Ed Swearingen was, technically, the first to apply the EGT concept to piston

engines—specifically, *radial* engines. "Ed was working on an autofeather system for Dee Howard's conversion [of the Ventura bomber into a business aircraft], and he had decided maybe measuring the exhaust temperature was the way to go. Cylinder head temperature was too slow to change, and you couldn't design an autofeather system around *that*. So he rigged up an EGT system and flew it. This was in 1959 or 1960, I think."

Al Hundere was also experimenting with EGT at the same time, as a way of finding a best-economy mixture setting in his Cessna 180, which he had been making long flights in (to South America, for example). "The airlines back then were leaning by cylinder temperature," Hundere explains, referring to the days when scheduled passenger service was via DC-6 or Boeing Stratocruiser. "The flight engineer, on long flights, would actually plot fuel consumption against cylinder head temperature while adjusting the mixture controls. On long flights, you had time to measure small CHT changes, and if you wanted the best fuel economy, you leaned by CHT. Well of course, in the Cessna you didn't have so much time to watch CHT. I wanted something faster, so I rigged up an exhaust probe wired to a big voltmeter in the cockpit. I think it was about a six-inch meter—I held it in my lap."

Alcor received the first STC (Supplemental Type Certificate) for installation of an EGT gauge—"but that was after we'd already installed a bunch of systems," Hundere explains. "We'd get requests from people in the local area, and I guess we must've installed a couple dozen systems before somebody, somewhere, got the idea that an STC was needed. Originally, we had gone to FAA's Southwest Region, and asked if we needed an STC, and they said 'Oh, heck no.' It was only later that we applied for, and got, an STC." That was in 1962. Since then, Alcor claims to have sold well over 125,000 EGT systems of various descriptions, for dozens of aircraft types.

Success was not immediate. In fact, as late as 1976, EGT systems were not standard equipment in most *turbocharged* airplanes, let alone normally aspirated ones, and Cessna was advising owners to lean as follows: "1. Pull mixture control out slowly until engine becomes rough. 2. Push the mixture control in slightly to obtain smooth engine operation; then enrichen further an equal amount." (From the 1976 Cessna Model 177B Cardinal *Pilot's Operating Handbook*.)

No one even knows what percentage of the fleet now is equipped with EGT instrumentation (although it is certain to be a high percentage—probably well over 50%). Most EGT systems tend to be of the single-probe variety, and almost all are retrofits—that is, installed by the owner, after-the-fact, rather than by the aircraft manufacturer. Also, most systems are installed on high-performance aircraft, not trainers. (Many trainers lack even cylinder head temperature instrumentation.) One consequence of this is that most student pilots today receive little or no instruction in the use of EGT systems. Advice on how to lean an engine is often summarized as: "Don't touch the mixture control below 5,000 feet. Above that altitude, pull it back until the engine runs rough, then enrichen slightly." Or: "On crosscountries, pull the mixture out a quarter of the way and leave it there." Since the average student tends to be a little trepidatious when it comes to touching the red knob that kills the engine at the end of every flight, many students just leave it alone, moving it only under the direct supervision of the instructor. (Is it any wonder training aircraft have such problems with spark plug fouling?)

Over the years, though, pilots have slowly, but surely, become more sophisticated with regard to mixture management. EGT manufacturers (and airframe manufacturers) have also advanced the state of the art, with multiprobe systems, fulltime all-cylinder instrument displays, and calibrated TIT (turbine inlet temp) systems for turbocharged engines. Some EGT gauges have a numeric liquid-crystal display; others use one or more analog needles; some "scan" the various cylinders one-by-one to detect temperature variations; and at least one manufacturer offers a gauge that reads CHT as well as EGT simultaneously, for all cylinders, while annunciating unwanted EGT excursions (due, for example, to mechanical malfunctions of individual cylinders). EGT systems—or "exhaust analyzers," as they are sometimes called—have thus become valuable troubleshooting tools, as well as "economy mixture indicators."

Unfortunately, the surfeit of information afforded by some of these gauges goes unused and unappreciated by many pilots. What good is a gauge that reads EGT (or TIT) accurately to within a degree Fahrenheit, if the pilot doesn't know how to interpret it?

Oddly, there are no books or manuals (aside from the occasional POH that discusses leaning by EGT) that pilots can turn to for guidance on EGT interpretation. The various EGT manufacturers offer technical literature on their products, but with the exception of Insight Instrument Corporation (makers of the Graphic Engine Monitor) and Alcor (which offers a useful booklet on exhaust analysis), none can be said to offer a truly comprehensive user's manual packed with "ground-zero" information on the combustion process. More than one manufacturer, in fact, actually offers faulty advice on combustion dynamics and mixture management. (Typical faulty claims are that the "hottest cylinder" and the "leanest cylinder" are the same; or that "best-economy EGT" occurs at peak EGT—which is only true for *some* engines, not all.)

Understanding how to use an EGT system requires a fairly substantial understanding of combustion dynamics—the how, why, and when of ignition, combustion, and heat transfer. This is especially true when it comes to troubleshooting (although even for basic leaning, it helps to know much more about the combustion process than can be gleaned from a cookbook-type chart).

The modern EGT has been likened to a "rectal thermometer for the engine." The analog is apt, because just as it helps to know something about human physiology and immunological processes before interpreting a thermometer, it helps also to know something about normal and abnormal combustion (and the Otto cycle) before one can expect to get the most out of an EGT system.

WHY MONITOR EXHAUST GAS TEMPERATURE?

A piston engine gets its power from controlled combustion of fuel and air. As everybody knows, in the combustion process fuel molecules recombine chemically with oxygen molecules from the air to give carbon dioxide, water vapor, and heat energy. Only a small portion of the total energy released in combustion is actually harnessed to do the work of moving the piston and crankshaft; by far the largest fraction of energy liberated in combustion goes out the exhaust pipe. (We should not be surprised by this. No combustion engine—including the human body—is more than 30 or 40 percent efficient in converting chemical energy into work.)

All internal combustion powerplants produce large volumes of hot exhaust. The purpose of an *exhaust gas temperature* system is to measure the temperature of the spent gases by means of a thermocouple-type probe in the exhaust pipe. While the absolute numeric value of the temperature of the exhaust is, in itself, of no particular significance (other than to indicate that the cylinder in question is in fact firing), the *manner* in which the exhaust temperature *changes* with alterations in

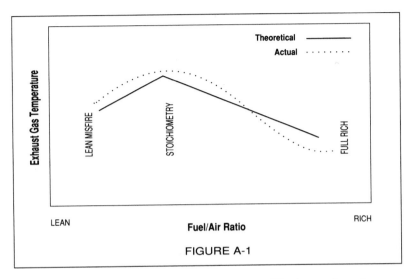

A plot of actual EGT versus fuel/air ratio gives a curve like the one shown here as a dotted line. In theory, the EGT "curve" should actually be a biphasic linear curve as shown by the solid line. Variations in cycle-to-cycle mixture strength, burn time, and heat conduction into the piston, valves, and cylinder head result in a real-world curve with a rounded peak. The actual value of peak will vary from engine to engine, and day to day (not to mention cylinder to cylinder).

throttle or mixture control is of great significance for determining the efficiency of combustion. Since combustion efficiency is profoundly affected not only by fuel/air ratio but by engine mechanical condition (piston blowby, valve leakage, advanced or retarded ignition timing, etc.), dynamic variations in EGT can tell the astute operator many important things about his or her engine. What's more, if probes are used to monitor EGT for *all* of an engine's cylinders, the operator has a valuable means of crosschecking the combustion efficiencies of each cylinder versus every other. This opens up whole new avenues for troubleshooting.

The *primary* signficiance of EGT monitoring for the average pilot, however (especially with single-probe systems), is in the determination of relative fuel/air ratios for leaning. As the mixture control is pulled back in flight, the fuel/air ratio in the cylinders goes from rich to lean, and at the same time, EGT goes from a lower value to a higher value, *then back to a lower value.* (EGT will, of course, abruptly become OAT if mixture is leaned too far!) These effects are shown in Figure A-1. When you first start to pull the mixture control back, EGT rises—

because combustion (or net heat release) is becoming increasingly efficient. More net heat energy is being liberated from the fuel because the chemical reactions of combustion are not being impeded by excess fuel molecules which are present when the mixture control is in the "full rich" position. At some point, as you continue leaning, the exhaust gas temperature will reach a peak (indicating that neither fuel molecules nor oxygen are present in chemical excess). As you lean even further, EGT will start back down, as fuel becomes the limiting ingredient in combustion. (Air is now present in excess.)

In Figure A-1 you can see an actual temperature curve from an aircraft engine operating in flight at 75 percent power. Along the vertical axis, EGT is plotted; fuel/air ratio (mixture control travel) is plotted horizontally. Notice that the curve is quite rounded on top. This rounded shape is quite typical for aircraft engines of all types. (The actual exhaust gas temperature may vary considerably from engine to engine, and cylinder to cylinder within an engine, but the shape of the curve is always the same.) The high point on the curve is called *peak* EGT. This is the optimum leaning point for many of today's engines. Some engines (usually those with turbochargers) cannot be operated at peak EGT; we will have more to say about those engines later. For now, it is important merely to know that the curve shown in Figure A-1 is broadly applicable to spark-ignition aircraft engines, regardless of make, model, or horsepower.

If you own a Lycoming engine and have looked at the applicable Lycoming Engine Operator's Handbook, or if you've ever consulted Lycoming Service Instruction No. 1094C, you've probably seen Lycoming's version of the graph in Fig. A-1, which is a little different from the version published here. Lycoming's graph of EGT versus fuel/air ratio shows straight-line variations in EGT leading to a rounded peak. The fact is that in a well-tuned high-compression engine (with cylinders running at nearly identical F/A ratios relative to one another), the EGT "curve" does, in fact, approach linearity on either side of peak EGT. In a *real* engine, however, cycle-by-cycle variations in mixture strength and combustion velocity (along with cylinder-by-cylinder variations in EGT due to mixture maldistribution) cause the EGT curve to be curvy, rather than linear, with a broad, flat peak. Oftentimes, as the mixture strength approaches the lean limit, EGT actually starts back up again (in real-world engines), although this effect is seldom important in mixture management. We will have occasion to discuss the implications of the curve shown in

Fig. A-1 many times throughout the course of this book. For now, it's enough to know that EGT increases as the mixture is pulled back; then, after peaking, EGT *decreases*. Usually, however, EGT does not follow a linear trajectory. The actual path is curved.

HOW IS EGT MEASURED?

In aircraft, exhaust gas temperature is measured with a small probe (approximately an inch long and 1/8-inch in diameter) inserted into the exhaust stack a few inches away from the combustion chamber. The sensing probe is a *thermocouple* sheathed in exotic "superalloy" material designed to withstand longterm exposure to corrosive, high-temperature exhaust gases. Inside the probe is a welded junction of two special alloy materials (namely, *chromel* and *alumel*); the junction of these two metals forms the thermocouple. In any junction of two dissimilar metals, the tendency of one metal to attract or donate electrons is always greater than the tendency of the other metal to attract or donate electrons—hence, when the two are joined, there is an electrical potential difference (that is, a tiny voltage) across the junction. This potential difference in turn varies with ambient temperature. That is to say, the junction develops increasing voltage as its temperature is raised. In an EGT probe, only 22 millionths of a volt are generated per degree rise (Fahrenheit). An EGT cockpit display can either be of the analog (needle movement) type, or digital. Analog gauges are basically voltmeters whose input is amplified and conditioned and then output as a needle reading. Digital gauges contain circuitry to convert the incoming analog voltage data into digital data that can be expressed in a variety of fashions—either numerically (on an LCD or LED display) or in some other fashion (such as bars or light-stacks, as in the Insight Graphic Engine Monitor). The digital display resolution may be one-degree (Electronics International), ten-degree (J.P. Instruments), or 25-degree F (Insight); but it's important to remember that the incoming data, in each case, is analog. The fact that a display head may read in 10- or 25-degree-F increments doesn't mean that the electronics inside aren't accurately measuring incoming data to fraction-of-a-degree precision. (See Chapter Eight.) Don't confuse instrument accuracy with display resolution.

Thermocouple pyrometry is an old and well-proven technology which is at the heart of many industrial and aerospace temperature-measurement applications today. In some EGTs, however, thermocouples are used to monitor much more than just temperature. The information provided by the probe can be used to monitor not only fuel/air mixture, but ignition timing, fuel distribution (or maldistribution), cylinder compression, and a host of other often-subtle, perhaps unexpected engine phenomena.

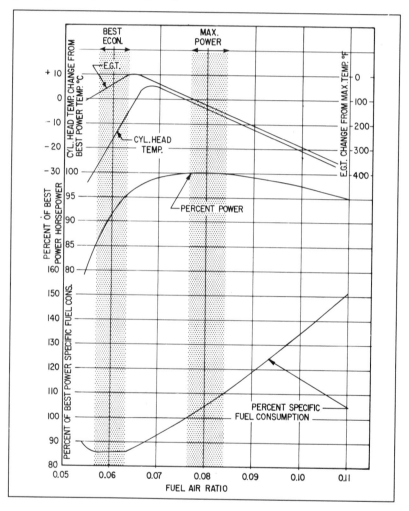

The Lycoming representation of Fig. A-1 has idealized curves for EGT and CHT, with linear ramping to and from peak. In the real world, EGT and CHT behave more like Fig. A-1. Lycoming's graph nonetheless summarizes the qualitative relationships between EGT, CHT, power, and specific fuel consumption accurately. Notice the relationship of peak CHT to peak EGT and peak power.

Virtually every EGT manufacturer relies on Type K thermocouples (i.e., thermocouples with a chromel/alumel junction; there are also Type J thermocouples, with an iron/constantan junction). Not all EGT probes are the *same*, however, in design, performance, or reliability. Differences in material and dimensional specifications, as well as construction (the use of heat barriers, for example, and potting compounds), lead to marked differences in thermal lag and MTBF (mean time between failures). An EGT probe may, depending on construction, last only a few hundred hours (or less!), or it may well go the life of the engine. Also, as we'll see later, the issue of "thermal lag," while potentially important, is not the critical issue in evaluating an EGT probe. (Thermal lag has to do not only with probe size—big probes taking longer to heat up—but also the *ratio of surface area to volume*.) In some EGT systems, probe response is seemingly "instantaneous," whereas in others it may take several seconds for a probe to respond visibly to a power or mixture adjustment. Obviously, if you're trying to determine EGT trajectories visually, yourself, without the aid of a computer, probe response matters, because a slow probe may take 10 or 20 seconds to move 50 degrees, and you haven't got all day to find peak EGT on the leanest cylinder. With an analog gauge especially, faster is better. But if you've got an instrument that can *interpret* EGT data *for you*, probe response needn't be a bottleneck—or even an issue worthy of discussion. It's easily possible, through clever software implementation, to have an instrument that *anticipates* probe thermal trajectories, essentially eliminating "probe lag" from consideration. (The first time-derivative of the temperature data gives this information.) To date, only the Insight GEM incorporates the necessary software to make this determination, allowing the near-instantaneous display of "target EGTs" well before probe equilibrium has been attained. The GEM has found widespread favor among high-end EGT users because it truly is an *interpretive* EGT—it analyzes data *for* the pilot. This way, the pilot doesn't *have to* determine his leanest cylinder visually (manually); the gauge will do it automatically. (Operation of the GEM is described in further detail in Appendix B.)

WHAT ABOUT
CYLINDER HEAD TEMPERATURE?

Today's modern aircraft engine is unique among internal combustion powerplants. The demands for small size, light weight, high power output, and overall excellent reliability place it in a class by itself. Unlike car engines, which are mostly small-displacement, high-revving, liquid-cooled engines with modest manifold pressure requirements, the engines used in today's light aircraft are large-displacement, slow-turning, air-cooled types which are customarily run at or near full throttle continuously, at altitudes ranging from zero to 25,000 feet and outside air temperatures ranging from well below zero (at high cruise altitudes) to well over 100 degrees, in certain arid regions. In an automobile, the operator may have a gauge (or annunciator light) for monitoring coolant temperature. The operator of a light aircraft has no "coolant" as such, and must therefore monitor cylinder head temperature (CHT).

The cooling requirements of an aircraft engine are worth pondering for a moment. An air-cooled engine receives cooling in three distinctly different ways. By far the most important form of cooling is that provided by ram air through the cowling. To take full advantage of this cooling airflow, cylinder heads are designed with large heat-exchange fins, and in some airplanes large controllable baffles (called cowl flaps) are provided on the cowling. In an air-cooled engine, lubricating oil also provides a certain degree of cooling (particularly in engines that incorporate piston oil cooling quirt nozzles); sometimes as much as 8% of the fuel energy passes to the oil. The heat carryoff to the oil of an aircraft engine is usually of a sufficiently severe magnitude to necessitate a separate heat exchanger for the oil (i.e., an "oil cooler").

Ram air and oil cooling are not sufficient, however, to prevent cylinder overheating in an aircraft engine at full power. An additional source of cooling, very important for suppressing detonation (or combustion knock) at high power settings, is the fuel itself. Excess fuel, over and above that needed to maintain efficient combustion, has a definite cooling effect on the cylinder head and associated components (valves, rings, etc.), and for this reason, air-cooled aircraft engines are designed to run extremely rich at full throttle—often as much as 50 percent richer than the "best power" fuel/air mixture.

Cylinder head temperature is monitored via a thermocouple mounted in a boss in the cast-aluminum cylinder head, generally near a spark plug. Temperatures in the region of the CHT probe are generally 300 to 400 degrees Fahrenheit in normal operation. (This compares with spark plug core temperatures of over 800 degrees and exhaust valve face temperatures of 1,000 degrees or more.) Engine manufacturers assign an arbitrary redline, or never-exceed, temperature of 460 to 500 degrees F to CHT for all current-production engines. When CHT exceeds these values, there is a likelihood that abnormal combustion (detonation, preignition) is occurring in the cylinder. Even if no abnormal combustion is occurring, it is possible for CHT to exceed redline if, for example, the aircraft is in an extended low-airspeed climb to high altitude. Regardless of cause, high CHTs are to be avoided, since the life of the cylinder head may be seriously compromised by the combination of severe thermal and mechanical stress.

The pilot has four ways of controlling cylinder head temperature. Cowl flaps, if available, provide more-or-less direct control over ram air flow through the engine compartment. (Accordingly, keeping cowl flaps open during takeoff, climb, or any time when high CHTs are encountered is standard operating practice.) The pilot also can control ram air cooling by changes in airspeed—e.g., lowering the nose and increasing the airspeed causes cooling to be improved and CHT to go down. A third method of controlling CHT is with the mixture control, since (as pointed out above) excess fuel has a direct evaporative cooling effect. A fourth and final method of CHT control is, of course, power reduction with the throttle.

It should be noted that most airplanes come new from the factory with only one CHT probe, connected to the cylinder that has been shown—by flight testing—to run hottest *in climb.* (Strictly speaking, FAA regulations do not require every airplane to come with a CHT gauge, and many training aircraft do not.) When you look at the original-equipment CHT gauge in a factory-equipped airplane, you are looking at CHT for *one cylinder only.* Abnormal combustion (from faulty injector nozzles, induction air leaks, etc.) may be occurring in other cylinders, but you have no way of knowing that by looking at the factory CHT gauge.

With an all-cylinder CHT gauge like the Graphic Engine Monitor 602/603, CHT indications for all cylinders are displayed simultaneously, on the same gauge (and at the same time) as EGT indications. As this book is being written, Insight is the only manufacturer that has brought an all-in-one, all-cylinder-realtime-display EGT/CHT gauge to market. Any significant change in CHT, for any cylinder, is immediately evident to the pilot (without any need to turn a selector dial or switch modes from EGT to CHT). Simultaneous digital display of CHT and EGT for all cylinders provides the pilot with the maximum information in minimal panel space, for easy interpretation and inflight troubleshooting.

EGT: THE KEY TO UNDERSTANDING YOUR ENGINE

The exhaust gas temperature gauge, whether of the single-probe variety or a more elaborate multiprobe setup, offers a unique glimpse into the internal combustion process. With an EGT, you can lean your engine precisely, confident in the knowledge that you are able to set the mixture so as to obtain the best fuel economy (if that is your goal), or the best horsepower for the given combination of manifold pressure and rpm, or the most efficient combustion in terms of efficient scavenging and low deposit buildup. In addition, the educated pilot is able, via EGT interpretation, to discern short- and longterm trend changes that might be indicative of mechanical problems ranging from ignition-timing discrepancies to valve burning, valve sticking, ring breakage, compression loss, injector nozzle clogging, etc. As a troubleshooting tool, EGT is without equal: A multiprobe EGT system can quickly pinpoint the location of combustion problems and provide valuable insight into the possible cause(s) of the malfunction. (All these aspects of EGT use will be addressed in the chapters that follow.)

It can truly be said that the pilot who understands EGT indications also understands his or her engine, and has the best chance of reaching TBO (the manufacturer's recommended Time Between Overhauls). Conversely, the operator who does *not* know how to interpret EGT or TIT stands a better-than-average chance of buying a top overhaul on the way to TBO—to say nothing of a lot of extra fuel that didn't need to be burned.

Study what this book has to say; return to it every few months; compare and contrast it to the advice given in your Pilot's Operating Handbook; compare and contrast it to your real-world experience as an EGT owner-operator. Chances are you'll find your understanding of aircraft engines has increased more than you thought possible. Meanwhile, your fuel economy will have gone up; your maintenance costs will have magically gone down; and your troubleshooting skill will (in all likelihood) place you in high esteem among your mechanic friends. In mastering the use of the EGT, you will have accomplished much more than learning how to use one instrument: You will have become a more capable, more responsible pilot.

Chapter 1

INTERNAL COMBUSTION FUNDAMENTALS

To get the most out of this book (and your EGT) requires that you have a thorough understanding of engine operating cycle concepts and terminology. We will be using terms like "intake stroke" and "expansion cycle" with fair regularity throughout the remainder of this

book, and as a result it is probably appropriate to take a moment now to review the basic components of the combustion process. We'll start with a detailed look at the *Otto cycle*. (If any term or abbreviation isn't self-evident, please refer to the Glossary at the back of the book. For now, we'll assume passing familiarity with such abbreviations as OAT, CHT, EGT, TIT, etc.)

THE OTTO CYCLE

All current-production aircraft engines (including the Dynacam engine), and virtually all automotive engines (whether of reciprocating *or* rotary design), operate according to the classic Otto cycle shown in Figure 1-1. (This cycle is named after its inventor, Nicolaus Otto, who perfected an engine based on it in 1876.) Engines that use the Otto cycle are often called *four-stroke-cycle* engines, since four strokes of the piston (two upstrokes and two downstrokes) are required to complete the cycle. On the intake stroke, the piston's downward motion creates a strong suction in the combustion chamber, which results in fuel and air entering the cylinder. (Air and fuel enter via an *intake valve*, which remains open for the entire stroke, closing after the piston has completed its downward travel.)

As the piston reaches bottom, the *compression stroke* begins. At this point, all valves—which is to say, the intake valve and the exhaust valve—are tightly closed and the combustion chamber, containing the air-fuel mixture, is sealed air-tight. With the piston coming back up, the combustion chamber volume of course decreases—meaning that

Figure 1-1

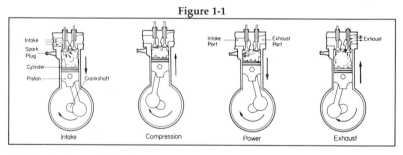

The classic Otto cycle (or four-stroke cycle) is composed of the intake, compression, power (or expansion), and exhaust events. This is an idealized account. In a real engine, ignition occurs late in the compression stroke; exhaust-valve opening (EVO) occurs about 60 degrees before the piston reaches bottom dead center (BDC) on the power stroke; and intake-valve opening (IVO) occurs at about 15 degrees before top center (BTC) on the exhaust stroke. (See text for discussion.)

the fuel-air charge is compressed. When the piston nears the top of the cylinder on the compression stroke, the spark plug (or plugs) discharges, igniting the fuel-air mixture. The resulting sudden gas expansion sends the piston down on the *power stroke.*

The power stroke is so named, of course, because it is the stroke on which the energy of combustion is delivered to the crankshaft, causing the crankshaft (and propeller) to turn over. During the power stroke, the valves remain closed, and the tremendous gas pressure produced during combustion causes the piston to move in the only direction in which its motion is unrestricted—namely, downward.

As the piston reaches bottom on the power stroke, the *exhaust valve* opens, allowing the hot combustion gases to begin to rush out of the cylinder. During the piston upstroke that follows, any remaining exhaust gases are physically pushed out of the combustion chamber by the piston. As the piston reaches the *top* of the exhaust stroke, the exhaust valve *closes*, the intake valve *opens*, and the entire cycle repeats itself.

How can a piston continue moving back and forth through four complete strokes when only one of those strokes actually develops power? Don't forget that in a four-cylinder engine, three other pistons are in various stages of the Otto cycle, all feeding their power into the same crankshaft. While one piston loafs, another pushes. Also, there's the momentum of the crankshaft and propeller to consider. (The flywheel effect of the propeller tends to keep things moving.) Actually, momentum effects are substantial enough to make three-cylinder, two-cylinder, and even *single*-cylinder Otto-cycle engines possible. While it seems an inefficient way of doing things at first, in reality it turns out to be a highly practical scheme. (There are also *two-stroke-cycle* engines, but we won't talk about those, since the planes built by Beech, Cessna, Piper, *et al* come only with four-stroke-cycle engines.)

The foregoing is actually a highly simplified description of the Otto cycle, of course. In a real engine, the various valve opening and closing events (and spark plug firing) do not coincide with piston reversal but are instead timed so as to optimize power production for a given set of conditions. In the typical Lycoming or Continental aircraft engine, for example, the intake valve doesn't open exactly at *top dead center* (TDC) of piston travel at the start of the intake stroke; actually it begins to open 15 degrees of crankshaft rotation *before* top center (BTC) of piston movement on the exhaust stroke. And as the intake valve is beginning to open, the exhaust valve (which was open on the previous stroke) stays open until 15 degrees *after* top center of the exhaust stroke. In other words, for 30 degrees of crank rotation, at the end of the exhaust stroke, both valves (intake and exhaust) are *open at the same time*. This is known as *valve overlap*. Because of gas inertia effects, a small degree of overlap actually aids exhaust scavenging while also improving intake-charge inflow. That is, the outrushing exhaust gases actually create a slight suction that tends to draw the intake charge in.

Likewise, the exhaust valve begins to open, in most Lycoming and Continental engines (others, too), not *at* bottom dead center on the power (or expansion) stroke, but about 60 degrees of crankshaft rotation *before* the piston reaches bottom center on the power stroke. (The technical term for this is *valve lead*.) Why should the exhaust valve open this early? Because for one thing, it takes a long time for exhaust gases to exit the combustion chamber; it helps to get an early start. For another thing, not much extra power is to be had by keeping the exhaust valve closed until BDC. The piston is connected to the crankshaft by means of a *connecting rod* whose angle to the crank *throw* (the offset piece of crankshaft to which it is attached) is always changing. It turns out that the amount of piston travel *per degree of crank rotation* is much less near the bottom of any stroke than the top or midpoint of any stroke. (See Fig. 1-2.) That is, the mechanical advantage of the piston over the crankshaft is very poor near bottom. It is a mechanistically inopportune time to try to extract work from the piston. It's also a thermodynamically inopportune time, as well, since combustion has long since ceased and the majority of gas expansion has already occurred.

The intake valve in a real-world engine opens (as we said) about 15 degrees early. It also closes about 60 degrees late. That is, the piston has already completed 60 degrees of crankshaft rotation on the *compression upstroke* before the intake valve actually closes. Again, this may seem counterintuitive, but there are good empirical reasons for "timing" the intake valve this way. Gas flow is not instantaneous; some time lag must be allowed if the maximum amount of fuel-air charge is to enter the cylinder on the intake stroke. Delaying the end of the intake stroke by keeping the intake valve open a little longer is a way of letting more fuel and air into the combustion chamber (just as delaying the start of the first act is a way of letting more theatregoers into the theatre before the play starts). Thanks to gas-inertia effects—and of course the fact that the piston doesn't actually *travel* very far per degree of crank rotation at the bottom of any stroke—the intake process is actually more efficient (more air is pumped by the cylinder) if in fact the intake valve is left open briefly after the intake stroke is complete.

The exhaust valve, then, opens 60 degrees early and closes 15 degrees late, while the intake valve opens 15 degrees early and closes 60 degrees late. The total valve-open time is thus about 255 degrees (180 degrees for the complete piston stroke, plus lead and lag angles) for either valve. Since the Otto cycle requires 720 degrees of crank rotation for the completion of all four events—intake, compression, combustion, and exhaust—it is easy to see that *each valve spends about two-thirds of its time closed*. (I.e., 255 divided be 720 equals roughly 1/3.) This information will be of importance later, when we talk about the EGT probe and what it actually "measures."

In a practical sense, valve timing

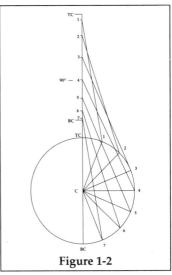

Figure 1-2

A one-to-one depiction of piston position (height) versus crankshaft angle shows that the piston actually travels much farther in the first 45 degrees of crank rotation (starting at top dead center, TDC) than in the last 45 degrees of the downstroke. Accordingly, the bottom of the power stroke is a poor time to try to extract energy from the combustion gases, and it makes sense to allow the exhaust valve to open early.

is of only academic interest to the pilot, since it cannot be controlled from the cockpit. The intake and exhaust valves are opened and closed by the action of a camshaft, which (in aircraft engines) is *gear-driven* straight off the crankshaft. There is nothing the pilot can do directly (and very little a mechanic can do, other than at overhaul time) to alter valve timing.

Some fairly rare types of engine distress, however, *can* throw valve timing off. For example, a collapsed lifter will reduce the valve-open time from 255 to perhaps 200, or even 180, degrees. (In most aircraft engines, valve-opening action is transmitted from the cam lobe to the pushrod and valve rocker by a small oleo-like device known as a *hydraulic lifter* or *tappet*. The hydraulic tappet's primary function is to take up slack in the valve train. Slack, or *lash*, occurs in valve trains because of the differential expansion of metals in the engine at high operating temperatures.) When a lifter collapses, or slack is introduced into valve-train components for *any* reason, the cam lobe must first overcome the clearances between parts in the valve train before the valve can be actuated; as a result, the valve opens slightly late—and closes slightly early. This might not sound terrribly harmful, but the effect on valve life, engine cooling, power output—and EGT and CHT—is nothing short of monumental. (These effects will be explored further in the chapter on troubleshooting.)

As an exercise, you might ask yourself what would be the consequences for efficient combustion if a valve—an exhaust valve, say— were to stick partway open, never entirely closing. (What would happen if an exhaust valve were to stick *closed?* An intake valve?)

IGNITION

Aircraft engines are, of course, *spark-ignition* engines. (There is also the *compression-ignition* engine, first perfected by Rudolf Diesel in 1892.) In a spark-ignition engine, the combustion event is precipitated by the sudden discharge of a spark (or two sparks, depending on how many spark plugs are present and operating) in the combustion chamber at precisely the right moment. The question arises, just what *is* the right moment? To this day, this is something that must be determined empirically by the engine manufacturer (i.e., tests are run using an actual engine whose ignition timing can be varied relative to piston travel). For most aircraft engines, sparking is timed to occur at 20 to 25 degrees of crankshaft rotation before the piston reaches top center on the compression stroke. This gives the best compromise of performance (horsepower vs. fuel efficiency) and cylinder cooling for most air-cooled aircraft engines operating in the 2,400 to 2,800 rpm range.

At first glance, you might think an engine would want to run backwards if the fuel-air charge were ignited at any point earlier than top center at the very beginning of the combustion (power) stroke. This is certainly true when it comes to *starting* an engine; for cranking purposes, you want ignition to occur fairly late—maybe even a few degrees *after* top center on the power stroke. (This is in fact accomplished on aircraft engines with the aid of special magneto accessories called impulse couplings.) When an engine is turning more than a few hundred rpm, however, *early* (or "advanced") ignition timing does not cause the engine to want to kick back or run the opposite way, because combustion *is not instantaneous*. When the spark plug discharges, a *flame front* is created near the plug's electrodes. This flame front spreads outward, in all directions, away from the spark plug (or away from each spark plug, if more than one is present and operating), at a fast—but finite—rate. Combustion is not actually complete until some time after the piston passes top center, even though combustion was *initiated* well ahead of that point.

Obviously, if combustion is initiated ridiculously early—or ridiculously late—in the compression/combustion cycle, the engine is not going to run properly (or at all). But between these extremes, it's possible to get an aircraft engine to run at any of various ignition timings in the zero to 60-degree BTC range. If one were to put an engine on a test stand and monitor specific fuel consumption (pounds of fuel burned per horsepower per hour) while varying ignition

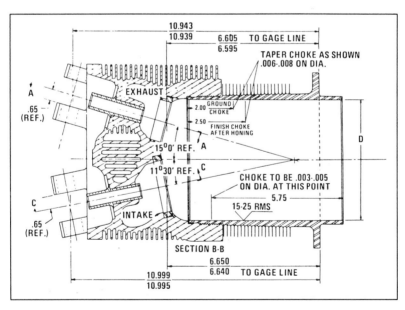

Drawing of an actual cylinder assembly shows dimensions in inches, angle between intake and exhaust valves (relative to centerline) in degrees, and choke (or barrel taper) specifications, in inches. Cooling fins on steel barrel are much thinner than on aluminum head. This type of head is referred to as an "angle-valve head" because of the fact that the valves are not parallel. Parallel-valve heads, although generally producing less power than angle-valve heads, are widely used in aircraft engines. Some engine families, such as the Continental O-470, incorporate both angle-valve and parallel-valve members.

timing, one would find that for a given rpm, there is one "best" ignition timing angle at which specific fuel consumption is lowest. For conventional aircraft engines operating in the 2,500 to 3,000-rpm range, the best-sfc timing is typically around 30 degrees BTC. (That's with two spark plugs per cylinders. With only one spark plug, combustion takes longer to complete, since one flame front must cover twice the distance. Hence, best-sfc timing with one ignition source might be 40 degrees BTC, or slightly more or less, depending on the combustion chamber size, geometry, and plug location.)

If you look at the metallic data plate on your Lycoming or Continental (or Franklin or Pratt & Whitney) engine, you'll see that the approved ignition timing for the engine is nowhere near 30 degrees BTC. It's more likely to be 20 or 22 degrees (or something similar). Setting your timing to anything other than 20 degrees (or whatever is indicated on your engine data plate) is illegal. Why don't the manufacturers allow us to time our engines for best fuel economy? Several reasons. The main reason has to do with cylinder cooling: CHT goes up dramatically as ignition timing is advanced beyond 20 or 25 degrees. If you *were* to advance your timing to 30 or 40 degrees, you'd have to operate at a richer mixture to keep your cylinders cool—thwarting any theoretical gain in sfc.

Advanced timing also reduces the detonation and preignition margins for your engine. (We'll have more to say about these destructive forms of combustion later on.) Also, greater stresses are put on cylinders and pistons, because the pressure spike after ignition becomes much "spikier" (if you will). The nominal, sea-level horsepower rating of your engine was determined at the timing shown on your engine data plate (in accordance with FAA type-certification rules). Advancing the timing beyond the data plate spec may well give your 260-hp engine 270 or 280 horsepower—an exigency for which it may or may not have been engineered. The combination of extra thermal and mechanical loadings will in all likelihood shorten your TBO—perhaps precipitously—while doing nothing good for CHT, oil temperature, or detonation margins. As one engine manufacturer was heard to remark, "Backing off on the timing a few degrees gives us a little bit less horsepower in return for much lower cylinder temperatures and greatly improved top-end life. It's a tradeoff that makes sense."

Unlike valve timing, *ignition* timing is of immediate, practical concern to pilots since spark timing does drift significantly in the course of an engine's life, due to normal wear inside magnetos (and abnormal maintenance at the hands of careless or ill-trained mechanics). This is one reason for doing the pretakeoff runup. Precisely *because* advanced timing gives a conservatively-timed engine more power, *the rpm drop on single-mag operation will be less for a magneto that has drifted "early" and greater for a mag that has drifted "late."* A very small mag drop, in other words—far from being something to brag about— is a tipoff to advanced timing (which could be due to premature breaker wear inside the magneto). A *large* mag drop, if not accompanied by engine roughness and/or a low EGT readout for one or more cylinders (indicating fouled plugs or bad lead wires), is likewise a tipoff to retarded, or late, timing.

We'll have more to say about the role of ignition timing in EGT and CHT indications in the chapters to follow.

FUEL AND AIR

For combustion to occur, obviously, there must be fuel, air, and an ignition source. Spark-ignition engines use (what else?) spark plugs for combustion initiation, but it is possible to get combustion without a spark. A red-hot engine deposit will initiate combustion under the right conditions, for example. Or mere compression of the fuel-air mixture (either by piston action, or some other action) can do the trick. From elementary physics, you know that compressing a gas causes it to heat up, while decompressing it causes it to cool down. Diesel engines exploit this fact to achieve combustion solely by compression of the fuel-air charge (eliminating the need for spark plugs altogether).

Spark or no spark, combustion will not occur unless fuel and air arrive in the cylinder in precisely the right amounts at precisely the right time. Since we live and breathe in a huge ocean of air, we take for granted the fact that oxygen is available to an engine in relative excess at all times; we tend to think of an automobile or airplane engine as something that primarily *burns gasoline*. In truth, an internal combustion engine primarily burns air! The fact is that for every part of fuel that goes into your engine, 10 to 20 parts of air must also go in. The volume flow involved is truly impressive. Consider a Continental IO-520 engine. The '520' in the designation means that the pistons of this engine displace a total volume of 520 cubic inches with every complete revolution of the crankshaft. At normal operating speeds, an IO-520 is pumping 500,000 cubic inches of air through its cylinders per minute! (Assuming 80-percent pumping efficiency, that is.) After an hour's flight, you may have burned only 15 gallons of gasoline, but you've consumed a whopping 2,326 gallons of air!

The fact that your engine is primarily an *air*-burner is reflected in the design of the throttle (the primary power-modulation control for any piston engine). The throttle does not control fuel flow. Take a look under your cowling and you'll see that your throttle is actually connected to an *air* valve in the throat of the engine. This air valve, often called a butterfly, is nothing more than a big disc-shaped plate of metal with a shaft through the diameter. The purpose of the butterfly is to vary the amount of air let into the engine. All spark-ignition aircraft engines, whether fuel-injected or carbureted, turbo-charged or normally aspirated, recip or rotary, are controlled by means of a throttle linked to a butterfly-type air valve.

The fact that your engine is an air-pumping device is also reflected in the design of the primary power gauge on the panel—the manifold pressure gauge. In a normally aspirated airplane, the manifold pressure gauge is really just a suction gauge connected to the intake manifold (the system of pipes leading to the intake ports of the cylinders). It reads in inches of mercury, just like a suction gage, and responds in a direct way to opening or closing of the engine's main *air* valve (the throttle), as you'd expect.

What, exactly, does a manifold pressure gauge measure? We mentioned earlier that fuel and air are drawn into the combustion chamber (via the intake valve) through the suction action created by the piston on its downstroke. Between the throttle butterfly and the intake valve for each cylinder is a system of pipes—the intake manifold—the air pressure in which can either be very near ambient (atmospheric) pressure, if the throttle is open, or very low if the throttle is closed. As the throttle is progressively closed, the pistons try in vain to aspirate (draw in) air past the blocked off throttle body. The partial vacuum that results is displayed as a low manifold pressure indication on the panel. At idle, your engine is trying to draw air past a virtually totally blocked off throttle throat, and manifold pressure can be as low as 12 inches of mercury on the "engine" side of the butterfly, even though on the upstream side of the butterfly the atmospheric pressure might be 29.92 inches of mercury. The exact manifold pressure (manifold suction?) indicated at idle will depend on how well-sealed your cylinders are. Obviously, a *high* MP indication at idle would be cause to suspect an induction air leak—or poor cylinder compression.

For now, the important thing to remember about manifold pressure is that the sensing line from the gauge always taps into the induction manifold at a point *downstream* (on the engine side) of the throttle butterfly—never upstream. This is true for turbocharged engines as well as normally aspirated ones.

Fuel is metered (that is, sent in appropriately measured doses) to the engine in response to *air-flow* changes caused by throttle adjustments. (By air-flow changes, I mean volume flow—not mass flow or density flow. Your carburetor or fuel injector knows nothing about the oxygen content of air passing through it—only volume flow is sensed.) Float-type carburetors of the sort used on single-engine Cessnas, and most other small aircraft, meter fuel on the basis of the pressure drop in a venturi—the magnitude of which is exactly proportional to air flow. Bendix fuel injection systems—such as, for example, used on a Lycoming IO-540—employ impact tubes and venturis to monitor air flow. The only type of system in widespread use that *doesn't* meter fuel in response to air flow is the Teledyne Continental fuel injection system used on IO-360, IO-470, IO-520, TSIO-, and GTSIO-series Continental engines. The TCM system meters fuel based primarily on engine *rpm*.

In an engine with a float carburetor, such as a Skylane's O-470-R or -U, fuel is discharged into the engine at a single point upstream of the butterfly valve. Gasoline emerging from the carburetor's main fuel jet sprays against the partially open butterfly, then must travel uphill—against gravity—to the cylinders via pipes several feet in length. Since the carburetor sits below and behind the engine, and the engine itself is several feet long, fuel droplets must travel much further to reach the most distant (furthest-forward) cylinders than to reach the ones nearest the carburetor. Fuel distribution, not surprisingly, is rather haphazard with this system. Some cylinders get significantly more fuel than others.

Fuel injection was devised as a means of obtaining more even (more precise and uniform) fuel delivery to the individual cylinders than is possible with carburetion. In a fuel-injected engine, gasoline arrives at the cylinder's intake port via a dedicated stainless-steel delivery line attached to a brass nozzle which screws into the cylinder head. Bendix and Continental fuel injectors are of the *continuous flow* type. This means that the injector nozzle sits *outside* the combustion chamber and sends a continuous flow of fuel (in a stream about the size of a mechanical-pencil lead) to the back side of the intake valve, *whether the valve is open or not.* "Continuous flow" means just that. The nozzle is *always squirting fuel*—even though, as we saw earlier, the intake valve spends approximately two-thirds of its time in the closed position.

Injector nozzles are carefully calibrated to ensure equal flow from cylinder to cylinder, and if kept unobstructed through frequent (100-hour) cleanings, these nozzles will indeed assure a precise flow of fuel to the cylinders. Nevertheless, the *fuel-air mixture will rarely, if ever, be exactly the same for each cylinder in an injected engine*, for the simple reason that bends and obstructions (and unequal distances) in the intake tubing virtually guarantee that some cylinders get more air than their neighbors. Admittedly, some engines are more carefully designed in this regard than others; for example, the air intake tubes on a Lycoming IO-540-A are of nearly equal length and curvature, whereas the induction-system design of a Continental IO-520-B has air traveling much farther to reach some cylinders than to reach others. (The IO-540-A is said to have better induction *tuning*.) This has important consequences for exhaust gas temperature.

When injector nozzles become obstructed, of course, radical changes occur in fuel flow and EGT (and CHT, quite often). Many plane-owners are not aware of the fact that nozzles require frequent cleaning to maintain optimum performance. If you check your aircraft service manual, you'll probably find that this is a recommended 100-hour inspection item. Still, most mechanics will not pull and clean injector nozzles unless specifically asked to, and airplanes generally come out of annual or 100-hour inspections with dirty nozzles. (The nozzles accumulate varnish-like fuel residues on the inside diameter after repeated hot shutdowns. Soaking the nozzles in acetone or methylethyl ketone removes the lacquer buildup and restores normal flow characteristics.)

As an aside, it should be noted that the fuel-flow indicator that comes as original equipment in fuel-injected airplanes is not really a fuel-flow indicator at all. The factory fuel-flow gauge is simply a pressure gauge plumbed to the flow divider (manifold valve; injector spider) atop the engine—the central valve or plenum from which the individual cylinder fuel-delivery lines emerge. Pressure at this point is proportional to total fuel flow *when all lines are free from obstruction*. If for some reason the delivery line (or nozzle) to one cylinder were to be blocked off, pressure at the flow divider would increase—and *indicated* fuel flow in the cockpit would go up (when actual fuel flow has, in reality, gone down). A sharp pilot, familiar with his or her plane, can readily spot a developing injector blockage problem on this basis. The average pilot, on the other hand, not only doesn't recognize the high fuel-flow indication as spurious but may actually lean the mixture to compensate for it—causing an already too-lean jug to become even leaner. (Of course, with any luck, if the cylinder is experiencing *severe* nozzle blockage, it will have been spotted on the ground during pretakeoff runup.)

THE COMPRESSION STROKE

One of the most important aspects of combustion in the classic Otto cycle is compression. The compression stroke has a far more important function than merely to allow the piston to return to top center for the start of the power stroke. Compression of the fuel-air mixture prior to ignition increases the efficiency of combustion, giving higher peak pressures (and more shaft horsepower) per unit of fuel consumed. Engines designed to maximize compression are more fuel-efficient, and generally more powerful, than engines with lower compression. This is the principle reason, for example, for the relative efficiency of diesel engines versus their spark-ignition counterparts.

When we speak of compression, we're really talking about two things: compression ratio (which is a design parameter of the engine), and actual cylinder compression (which varies from cylinder to cylinder and day to day, depending on valve sealing, ring tolerances, and the like).

Compression ratio is the ratio of combustion chamber volume with the piston at the *bottom* of its travel to the volume with the piston at *top center* in its travel. (*Displacement* is the difference between these two volumes.) The combustion chamber volume with the piston at the top of its travel is surprisingly small. If you know the compression ratio (C.R.) and overall displacement of your engine, you can calculate the clearance volume rather easily by dividing C.R.-minus-one into the cylinder displacement. For example, we know that an IO-520 has six cylinders and displaces a total of 520 cubic inches, so each cylinder must displace 520 divided by 6, or 86.7 cu.in. We also know (from looking at the engine data plate) that a normally aspirated IO-520 has a compression ratio (C.R.) of 8.5-to-one. Subtracting one from C.R. gives 7.5; and dividing 7.5 into 86.7 gives us the clearance volume of an IO-520: namely, 11.6 cubic inches. (The combustion chamber volume at the bottom of piston travel is 11.6 *plus* 86.7, or 98.3 cubic inches.)

When you stop to think about the fact that the piston diameter of an IO-520 is 5.25 inches, eleven cubic inches is a remarkably *tiny* volume in which to conduct combustion in a 285-hp engine. In fact, this puts the piston so close to the top of the combustion chamber that it is in definite danger of being struck by a valve, should a valve not close completely. (Some pistons for high-compression engines are de-

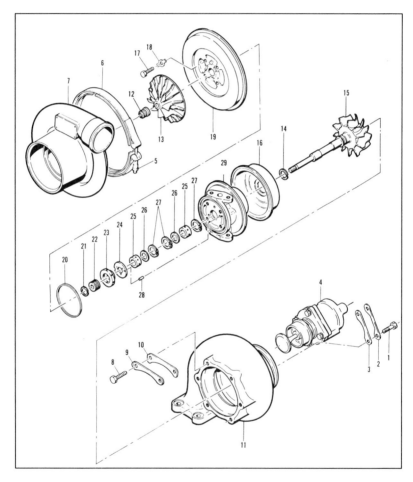

The modern turbocharger consists of an exhaust turbine rotor (15) on a common shaft with a compressor wheel (13). The engine's exhaust turns the rotor and causes massive quantities of air to be blown into the engine's intake system via the compressor. Turbo output is controlled by a wastegate. The particular model shown (an AiResearch TH08A, used on the Pressurized Navajo and others) incorporates a poppet-valve wastegate (4). Because of the extra back-pressure imposed on the exhaust system, turbochargers tend to run hot and make the engine run hotter as well.

signed with scooped-out areas or impressions on the piston dome, for just this reason.)

Notice that compression ratio and displacement are independent design parameters: You can easily change compression ratio (by using taller pistons, for example) without altering displacement. And in fact, most turbocharged aircraft engines are designed to have a lower compression ratio than their normally aspirated counterparts.

For example, all TSIO-520 Continentals have a compression ratio of 7.5-to-1 (achieved by use of different pistons), while IO-520 engines have a C.R. of 8.5-to-1. (This gives the TSIO-520 a clearance volume of 13.3 cu. in.)

Why do turbocharged engines generally employ a lower compression ratio? Actually, if you count the output of the turbocharger compressor as part of the engine's overall "compression ratio," you of course find that the TSIO-520 operates with an effective C.R. well above the IO-520's. A lower compression ratio is used in turbocharged engines to provide an extra margin of detonation suppression. One of the problems of operating at a high compression ratio is that the fuel-air mixture, when vigorously compressed, has a tendency to self-ignite before the spark plug gets a chance to do its job. You'll recall that when a gas is compressed, it becomes heated. The heat of compression, combined with the heat from already-sizzling-hot cylinder components, is enough to make controlled combustion very difficult in a spark-ignition engine at compression ratios much above nine or ten to one.

Even at compression ratios below 10-to-1, detonation can be a serious problem, depending on the quality of the fuel. Detonation, or combustion knock, happens *after the spark plug fires*. (Remember, there is a special name for combustion that happens *prior* to the firing of the spark plug: viz., preignition.) Detonation occurs when the compression of the *unburned* fuel-air mixture by the *burning* (and expanding) fuel-air mixture results in the spontaneous, explosive combustion of the unburned charge. That is, no sooner does the spark plug ignite the fuel-air mixture, and the mixture begins to burn, than the whole thing lights off—all the fuel molecules decompose and release their energy—all at once. When this happens in a car, the result is a pinging or clattering sound (knocking). When it happens in an airplane, you generally can't hear anything unusual above the normal racket of the engine and propeller. Your first indication of a problem may not come until CHT hits redline, or a connecting rod falls in your lap. Careful combustion-chamber design can do a great deal to stave off detonation at high compression ratios. For example, cylinders with hemispherical combustion chambers and angled valves (instead of parallel valves) are knock-resistant to much higher compression ratios than other engines. The same is true of engines that use two spark plugs per cylinder. Operation on a single magneto will leave you with less detonation margin than before. Another means of coping with detonation is to use a knock-resistant fuel—i.e., a higher-octane gasoline. Commercially available gasolines with an octane rating higher than that found in 100LL avgas are rare, however, so in the end, the aircraft-engine designer must be content to design knock resistance into the engine by keeping compression ratios well below 10-to-1 and employing retarded timing, generous fuel cooling, and (where possible) low manifold pressures and rpms.

Of course, for compression of the fuel-air mixture to occur at all in an engine, the combustion chamber must be tight to begin with—no big leaks anywhere when the valves are closed. When valves fail to seal properly or piston rings become worn (or broken), fuel and air will leak out of the combustion chamber prior to spark-plug firing, and combustion—if it occurs—will be anything but energetic. The so-called differential-compression test (which you've probably seen your mechanic do at annual or 100-hour inspection time) is a method of detecting leaky cylinders. Basically, the differential compression test is set up in such a way that any cylinder with more than 25-percent leakage at a static pressure of 80-psi will flunk the test. The methodology has its drawbacks, but the point is well taken that any cylinder that has significant leakage past valves or rings can be expected to perform poorly in the course of normal operation.

How does compression relate to exhaust gas temperature? In a leaky cylinder, combustion is less efficient—peak temperatures are lower—and EGT is less, all other things being equal. A Baron operator of our acquaintance, on his very first flight after installation of an Insight Graphic Engine Monitor, was able to diagnose a cylinder with broken rings in this fashion. Had he not installed the GEM when he did, this operator may have continued to operate the aircraft for some time before discovering the bad cylinder on a compression test.

TURBOCHARGING

In theory, the power output of a spark-ignition piston engine is limited only by the amount of air-and-fuel that can be crammed into the combustion chamber(s) during each intake event. Since fuel delivery is a relatively simple matter (mechanistically speaking), the real problem is how to get more air into the engine. One way of getting an engine to breathe more air is to use a pump or air compressor to force air into the intake system. This concept, broadly speaking, goes by the name *supercharging*.

A turbocharger is a subclass of supercharger. (In fact, turbochargers are sometimes called *turbosuperchargers*—hence the 'TS' in TSIO-520.) The "turbo" in turbocharger comes from the fact that the device is driven by a *turbine* wheel which is located in the engine exhaust and spun to high speed by outrushing exhaust gases. Put a turbine wheel on a common shaft with a centrifugal air compressor, and you have a turbocharger. (See Figure 1-3.)

Modern turbochargers are remarkably efficient in converting exhaust energy to manifold pressure. (It could also be said that piston aircraft engines are remarkably efficient in converting gasoline into waste heat; one statement goes hand in hand with the other.) In fact, fairly careful engine and turbocharger-system design is necessary to prevent even a small turbocharger from pumping so much hot air into an engine that it knocks. And even then, a considerable degree of operator training and knowledge is called for to obtain maximum performance and reliability from a turbocharged powerplant.

Turbocharging brings with it many interesting and important design considerations where valving, compression ratio, ignition timing, fuel delivery, and operator controls are concerned. Take valving, for example. In a normally aspirated engine, the intake valve face is normally quite a bit larger than the exhaust valve face. Why? Because a normally aspirated engine has a much harder time taking in air than it does blowing out hot, high-pressure exhaust gas. In a turbocharged engine, by contrast, exhaust valves and intake valves are often nearly the same size. (Also, the camshaft lobe profile may differ significantly with respect not only to lift and duration but valve overlap as well.)

The compression ratio of turbocharged engines (as explained earlier) is often less than that of unturbocharged engines, to provide extra detonation protection. Ignition timing is usually set back a few degrees—to 20 degrees BTC from 25, for example—also, for the same reason.

Fuel injector nozzles present a special problem. All injector nozzles in current use employ an air-bleed hole, vented to the engine compartment. In a normally-aspirated engine, engine-compartment air is always at a higher pressure than intake-manifold air, so the bleed hole in the nozzle acts to aid aeration or atomization of the fuel spray—in theory. (In reality, a relatively large delta-p across the bleed orifice is required to produce any atomization at all, and at power settings above a fast idle, no atomization occurs.) In a turbocharged engine, manifold pressure is frequently higher than engine-compartment pressure, which means that fuel will spray out the nozzle orifice (into the hot engine compartment) if the nozzle is merely vented to ambient air. If you study a turbocharged engine you'll notice that the fuel injector nozzles have their own air manifold; each nozzle is shrouded and vented to high-pressure turbo air ("deck" air).

In recent years it has become popular to apply pressurization to the magnetos of turbocharged aircraft (via a system of tubes and fittings similar to those used to bring turbo air to injector nozzles). Magneto pressurization is simply a way of reducing mag misfire at high altitude; compressed air acts as a dielectric, suppressing the stray jump-gap arcing that might otherwise occur in the rarefied air of the upper atmosphere. Many turbocharged aircraft now come with pressurized magnetos, including the Piper Malibu, Navajo Chieftain, Mooney 231, Cessna T210, P210, and T303, and RAM-modified Cessna twins. (Retrofit kits are also available for the Piper Turbo Arrow, Seneca II and III, Turbo Lance, Cessna TU206, and others.) Magneto pressurization has done a good job of reducing high-altitude misfire in these aircraft (and has probably prevented much engine damage), but—like fuel nozzle shrouding—it adds yet another layer of complexity to an already-complex firewall-forward picture.

Compressed air from a turbocharger is hot (often as much as 250 degrees Fahrenheit), and in the absence of special cooling efforts the heat of compression gets passed directly to cylinder heads and valves, fuel nozzles, magnetos, and anything else "vented" to the compressor outlet. This reduces detonation margins (not to mention engine cooling margins), and to compensate, the pilot of a turbocharged engine must often operate with cowl flaps open and/or use a relatively rich mixture in high-altitude cruise. A popular method of reducing the BTU burden on highly boosted engines is to install an air/air heat exchanger (radiator) in the induction system between the compressor outlet and the throttle-body (or injector body). This scheme goes by the name *intercooling*, a word that owes its origin to the fact that the first such devices were interposed *between* supercharger stages in the highly boosted radial engines of World War II military aircraft.

Relatively few general aviation aircraft come with intercooling as standard equipment (the Cessna T210, P210, and 414A, and Piper's Malibu, are exceptions), but aftermarket kits are readily available for many aircraft.

Since every turbocharger is capable of providing destructive levels of boost, some means must be provided for maintaining manifold pressure within acceptable limits. The most direct means of controlling the turbocharger's output is to vary the amount of exhaust gas directed to the turbine. This is done with (usually) a butterfly-type valve called a *wastegate*, which—depending on the particular installation—may be controlled manually by the pilot, or controlled automatically via hydraulic actuators linked to various bellows arrangements. In some aircraft (e.g., Turbo Skylane, Turbo Saratoga) the wastegate is mechanically linked to the throttle. In others (Turbo Arrow, Mooney 231), there is no wastegate butterfly at all; instead, a built-in exhaust leak ahead of the turbocharger diverts a certain (fixed) fraction of the exhaust gases to the turbine while dumping the remainder overboard. Most systems (regardless of the type of wastegate control) also include a poppet-type pressure relief valve in the intake system to prevent serious engine damage in the event of a sudden surge in turbo output (pilot-induced or otherwise). Pressure relief valves are not foolproof, however. Most turbocharged engines can be overboosted if the pilot tries hard enough (sometimes even *without* trying).

With the wastegate open (and the turbo effectively taken off-line), a turbocharged engine behaves the same as a normally aspirated engine in most respects. At high altitudes, however, with the wastegate closed (and all, or nearly all, exhaust gas flowing through the turbocharger), the boosted engine is a different animal. A closed control loop is formed such that any increase in mass flow through the turbine results in an increase in compressor output, which may trigger a rise in fuel flow, which increases mass flow through the turbine, etc. The feedback effects are further magnified by ram recovery (which on some planes, such as the Cessna twins, can be very significant). In a dive, many turbocharged airplanes (and some non-turbocharged planes, too, of course) will pick up manifold pressure. The pressure rise at the airscoop is multiplied by the pressure ratio of the compressor, which at 18,000 feet is apt to be 2.0 or more, so that what would be a one-inch "ram rise" in MP for a normally aspirated plane becomes a two-inch MP excursion for the turbocharged aircraft. Any increase in manifold pressure in turn increases mass flow through the turbo-charger, which increases compressor output, which increases power and airspeed, etc. What this means for the pilot is that many iterations may be needed to set the plane up properly (with respect to manifold pressure, fuel flow, rpm, pitch trim, etc.) for high-altitude cruise, since any one variable now affects all the others.

As we will see in the next chapter and throughout this book, the special performance characteristics of turbocharged engines give rise to some unexpected considerations for leaning and cruise operation. For turbocharged operators in particular, a full multiprobe, multidis-play system like the Insight GEM can pay big dividends, not just in fuel savings, but maintenance savings (and inflight peace of mind) as well.

Chapter 2

PRINCIPLES
OF MIXTURE
MANAGEMENT

EGT systems were first developed for (and to this day are primarily used for) accurate leaning. And yet, after 30 years of EGT retrofits, pilots remain largely ill-informed when it comes to mixture manage-

ment. Why does an engine become richer at high altitudes? Why doesn't the carburetor compensate for the thinner air? The answer is, the carburetor (or fuel injector) doesn't know what the oxygen concentration of incoming air is. Aircraft fuel-metering systems meter fuel based on volume flow, or pressure changes in a venturi—not based on air density. At 23 inches of manifold pressure and 2,300 rpm (to give an arbitrary example), your engine is being delivered a particular fuel flow—say 10 gallons per hour—with the mixture in "full rich." With the throttle set for "23-square" your engine will receive the *same* fuel flow at sea level as at 2,500 feet or 4,000 feet, or 6,000 feet (assuming you can still get 23-square at 6,000 feet, that is). Yet, the air density is only 80 percent of sea-level at 6,000 feet; so your engine will be almost 25 percent richer at 6,000 than at sea level. Your engine will run richer and richer the higher you go, unless you have a way of leaning it out.

Temperature has an important effect on air density (as any pilot who has heard about "density altitude" knows); the hotter the air, the thinner it is. Thus, even at sea level, your effective mixture will change from day to day based on OAT and density-altitude effects.

Even if atmospheric oxygen content were the same for all altitudes (and all temperature conditions), you'd still want to have a mixture control. Why? Because your engine is set to run super-rich at takeoff—for cooling purposes, as well as to suppress detonation. After you throttle back (to 23-square, or whatever) for cruise, you no longer need to run super-rich. Even at sea level, you'd want to be able to lean the engine for cruise.

We'll take a look at leaning for cruise, climb, and other flight conditions later on in this chapter. But before we go any further, we need to define our terms and make sure we know what we're talking about when we speak of things like combustion, fuel/air ratio, "best power" mixture, "best economy," etc. We'll start with the concept most fundamental to engine operation: combustion.

Combustion is the autocatalytic (self-sustaining) decomposition of a fuel (such as gasoline) in the presence of oxygen to give carbon dioxide, water, and energy (heat and light; chiefly the former). The chemical rearrangement of fuel and oxidizer to give oxidized reactants, energy, and water (steam) is central to *all* combustion.

The energy that results from combustion is, of course, not created out of nothing—it was there to begin with in the chemical bonds of the reactant molecules. When the reactant molecules (fuel, oxygen) interact, they break apart and recombine atoms to form compounds (CO_2

This Alcor left/right EGT display (for twins) is unusual in having numeric calibration marks. Strictly speaking, numbers are not necessary unless the probe is of the TIT (turbine inlet temp) type. Particular EGT temperatures are of no significance for leaning, except in relation to peak EGT.

and H_2O) that have lower-energy bonds than the original reactants. The release of energy in this process sends atoms, molecules, and fragments of molecules (called *radicals*) flying apart at great velocity; radicals and molecules colliding with other radicals and molecules causes the combustion process to be self-sustaining once it gets underway. The process continues until there are no unreacted high-energy molecules left. In the end, "stable" (unreactive, inert) end-products are all that's left—along with a great deal of heat.

Of course, merely bringing fuel and oxygen together doesn't cause a fire, any more than putting a car at the top of a hill causes it to speed away by itself; an initial "nudge" must be imparted to the reactants (i.e., a spark or flame must be provided) to get combustion to begin.

In principle, any exothermic reaction that yields oxidized byproducts could qualify as "combustion," but in order for internal combustion as we know it to occur in an engine, it is essential to have fuel, air (oxygen), compression, *and* an ignition source (i.e., a spark) present in the combustion chamber *in the right proportions*, and *at the right time*. Too much or too little fuel will cause combustion to fail just as surely as taking away the source of ignition will. For power to be produced by the engine, ignition must occur in a fairly narrow range of crankshaft positions—create a spark too early or too late, and the engine stops. Likewise, if you alter compression (by allowing a hole in the combustion chamber, for example), power production is affected in fairly dramatic fashion. These sorts of factors were discussed briefly in Chapter 1.

Not just any fuel will do for an internal combustion engine. The fuel should be as energy-rich as possible—which in chemical terms means it should be in a highly reduced (easily oxidizable) state, rich in hydrogen. For convenience sake it should also be easily dispensed and transported, and if possible, cheap to produce. The general family of compounds known as hydrocarbons qualify in most of these respects. Methane, ethane, propane, butane, various alcohols (including drinking alcohol), aromatics such as benzene and toluene, coal and shale products, and wide-cut petroleum distillates (such as gasoline and kerosene) have all been used as fuels with excellent success.

Gasoline, it turns out, is a very energy-rich assortment of molecules, as liquid hydrocarbon fuels go. A single gallon of gasoline, in fact, contains about 112,000 BTU of energy—enough to heat a bathtub full of ice-water to the boiling point. (Ethyl alcohol, by comparison, yields only 78,000 BTU per gallon—still enough for a warm bath, but not nearly as good as gasoline.)

Kerosene and jet fuel are about as energy-dense as gasoline, but unfortunately these fuels cannot be used in spark-ignition aircraft engines because of their abnormal combustion qualities (in terms of poor antiknock or "octane" performance). Using Jet A in a Lycoming or Continental engine is a sure way to induce detonation and subsequent engine failure.

Gasoline is not an easy substance to characterize chemically— because it is *not* one substance, but a mixture of many different chemical components (numbering in the hundreds). Because gasoline is not a chemically uniform fuel, we cannot speak, for example, of gasoline as having a well-defined boiling point. The constituent hydrocarbon species that make up gasoline have their own individual boiling and freezing points—the lighter-weight species tend to want to vaporize and boil first—but to make generalizations is difficult. One thing we *can* say is that it takes a relatively large quantity of oxygen to fully oxidize or react with (combust; turn to carbon dioxide and water) a small amount of gasoline. In fact, it takes approximately 3.37 pounds (or mass-equivalents) of oxygen to completely burn one pound (or mass-equivalent) of gasoline. Anything less than 3.37 pounds will leave some gasoline still unburned. Anything more will leave an excess of oxygen.

Of course, air is not 100-percent oxygen; in fact it is only 21 percent oxygen. Thus, dividing 3.37 by 0.21 gives the correct mass ratio of *air* to gasoline, namely 16. You need 16 pounds of air to completely burn one pound of gasoline. This is what a chemist would call the *stoichiometric* ratio of the reactants. ("Stoichiometry" refers to chemical balance; stoichiometry is the bookkeeping side of chemistry.) An air/fuel ratio of 16:1 (a fuel/air ratio of 0.067) is chemically ideal, since neither air nor fuel is present in excess.

The correct (stoichiometric) air/fuel ratio for combustion will vary somewhat from fuel to fuel depending on the chemical nature of the fuel. Obviously, a fuel such as methyl alcohol (CH_4OH), which already contains an oxygen atom in the chemical formula, will not require as much air (oxygen) for combustion as a pure hydrocarbon, and the stoichiometric A/F ratio will be lower. (Also, the energy released on combustion will be lower.) Even with gasoline, the ideal A/F ratio will vary slightly from batch to batch, since not every batch of gasoline contains the exact same mix of ingredients. Industry specs put a limit on the minimum BTU content of a gallon of avgas (ref. ASTM D-910), but the latent heat content of automobile gasoline can vary significantly, especially when adulterated with alcohol to give "gasohol." If you have occasion to operate your plane on autogas, you should bear this in mind. An energy-poor (oxygenated) gasoline blend will shift your effective A/F ratio in the lean direction, resulting in a slight increase in takeoff EGT.

It is possible to get combustion to occur inside an engine at air/fuel ratios from 8:1 to as high as 18:1, given appropriate encouragement in terms of spark and pressure. When an excess of either air *or* fuel is present initially, however, combustion is not as efficient—the fire isn't as quick to burn—because the overabundant species inhibits catalysis and slows the reaction rate.

Below a certain threshold rate, the reaction is not self-sustaining, and combustion ceases. By far the most efficient release of energy occurs when neither fuel nor air is present in excess. For this reason, a stoichiometric air/fuel mixture gives the highest exhaust gas temperature—what we commonly refer to as peak EGT.

It is important to have some idea of the magnitudes of the temperatures and pressures encountered in an aircraft engine's combustion chamber. Peak temperatures on the order of 4,000 to 5,000 degrees Fahrenheit are common, while peak pressures are in the range 400 to 800 psi, or 800 to 1,600 inches of mercury. (A lot depends on compression ratio, manifold pressure, and leakage past rings and valves, naturally.) Average temperatures and pressures are much lower, of course, since the combustion event is of relatively short duration vis-a-vis the total Otto cycle. Nonetheless, the temperatures and pressures involved are impressive. Moreover, they are directly under the pilot's control.

THE EFFECT OF FUEL/AIR RATIO ON EGT

You alter the fuel/air ratio directly every time you move the mixture control in the cockpit, of course, with profound (or potentially profound) consequences for exhaust gas temperature, turbine inlet temperature, cylinder head temperature, fuel flow, exhaust emissions, and quite possibly overall engine life. For purposes of best EGT use, it is essential that you understand the effect of F/A-ratio changes on exhaust gas temperature. (Please do not skip over this part of the book, even if you have already been exposed to the basic concepts before. Many of the basic concepts have been incorrectly explained elsewhere.)

The effect of mixture changes on EGT is depicted in Fig. 2-1 (and Fig. A-1 in the Introduction). Also shown here are curves for CHT, relative percent power, and specific fuel consumption, plotted with fuel/air ratio on the abscissa (horizontal axis) and temperature on the ordinate (vertical axis). Notice how EGT rises, peaks, and falls off again as the mixture is retarded from full-rich to something approaching full-lean. Notice also the fact that the CHT and relative power curves also peak in a similar fashion, but with none of the peaks coming at the same F/A ratio. The EGT, CHT, and power curves peak at different points.

The sharp reader will want to know whether the F/A adjustments made in Fig. 2-1

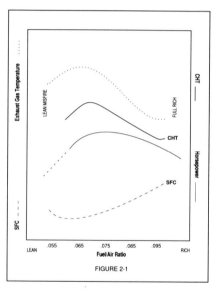

FIGURE 2-1

The relationships of EGT, CHT, horsepower, and sfc (specific fuel consumption) to fuel/air ratio—and to each other—are shown qualitatively on this graph, which replicates Lycoming's graph (Fig. A-2, Introduction) but is closer to real-world results. The actual shapes of the curves will vary somewhat from plane to plane, but the positions of peak CHT, peak EGT, and peak horsepower vary little between engines. Specific fuel consumption may bottom further to the left (to the lean side) in high-compression, angle-valve cylinders.

were accomplished by varying the fuel flow, or varying the air flow. After all, F/A ratio can be changed in either way. (It makes a difference in the shape of the curves, too.) The answer is, the graph is plotted for a *constant throttle setting*, which is tantamount to constant air flow. The fuel/air ratio, in other words, has been varied by retarding the mixture control. The graph thus duplicates the conditions encountered in the real world, and can be applied to real-world situations.

Does Fig. 2-1 have general significance to all types of aircraft, regardless of engine model? Yes. The *absolute* values of EGT, CHT, and s.f.c. will of course vary from engine to engine, and even from cylinder to cylinder within a given engine (and day to day for a *given cylinder* within a given engine), but the shapes of the curves, and their relationships to each other, are broadly applicable to a wide range of aircraft.

It's worth pointing out also that Fig. 2-1 is really a graph for just one cylinder, and because of differences in induction tuning and fuel delivery from cylinder to cylinder (resulting in some jugs running leaner than others), the curves for other cylinders on the same engine might be skewed a little to the left or right. Still, the overall shapes of the curves and relationships of the peaks would be the same.

In discussions of this sort, it is customary to explain the fall-off of EGT on the lean side of peak as being due to "air cooling" from the excess of air entering the combustion chamber. In reality, combustion occurs more slowly at lean mixture settings, and—all other things being equal—one might well argue that indicated EGT should stay constant or even *increase* slightly at mixtures leaner than peak, since late combustion usually means a less-well-cooled slug of exhaust out the exhaust port. The answer is that EGT decreases as the pilot leans beyond peak because he or she is introducing less fuel to the fire. You are lowering the F/A ratio by decreasing fuel flow (not by increasing the air flow); temperature naturally goes down. This only stands to reason. Put less fuel in the combustion chamber, and you get fewer BTUs out the exhaust pipe.

On the rich side of peak, of course, you have unburned fuel galore— an excess of fuel molecules roaming aimlessly around the combustion chamber searching (in vain) for oxygen molecules with which to interact. The net effect in this case is, in fact, a cooling or quenching of the reaction. The excess fuel has a direct cooling effect. EGT on the rich side of peak is less, as a result.

In a turbocharged engine with the wastegate closed, the curves shown in Fig. 2-1 will not take exactly the same shape—the EGT peak will be broader, as will the CHT peak, and the power curve will peak further to the right. This is because as the mixture is retarded in high-altitude cruise (with the throttle locked), overall flow through the turbocharger decreases, the turbo spins down to a lower rpm, manifold pressure dips, and power falls off, due to the closed-feeback-loop effects described at the end of Chapter One. At low altitudes, however, with the wastegate open, Fig. 2-1 will be very nearly the same for a turbocharged engine as for a normally aspirated one.

What is the significance of "peak EGT" (and adjacent operating regions) for overall engine performance? Well for one thing, you can see from Fig. 2-1 that it is possible to set the mixture in such a way as to provide either maximum power, or maximum fuel economy, solely by reference to EGT. How? The first step is always to find peak EGT. Regardless of the make or model of EGT, or how many probes, the way to do this is simply to pull the mixture knob out slowly while observing the EGT gauge. It's best to do this in small increments: pull the mixture back a millimeter or two, wait five or ten seconds, note the EGT, pull the mixture back some more, etc. The EGT will eventually reach a maximum, then start back down as you continue leaning. When EGT is at the maximum, you are by definition "leaned to peak." (With the Insight GEM, whose operation is discussed further in Appendix B, finding peak EGT is a simple matter of leaning the mixture with the instrument in Lean Mode and waiting for the leanest cylinder EGT readout to begin flashing, telling you that that particular cylinder has reached, or even gone slightly beyond, peak. Of course, peak EGT can also be found manually, for any cylinder, by simply observing each EGT readout as the mixture is slowly leaned.)

With a multiprobe EGT, it is possible, obviously, to find peak EGT for the individual cylinders; rarely will they all peak at the same time (or at the same temperature). It is customary to lean by reference to the *leanest cylinder*—the cylinder that reaches peak EGT first on leanout—rather than by reference to the hottest cylinder or richest cylinder (or some other cylinder), since the leanest cylinder will be the first to "cut out" or suffer lean misfire as leaning is continued. If you lean by reference to any but the leanest cylinder, you may encounter engine roughness when attempting to find peak EGT on other cylinders. (The roughness isn't necessarily harmful in and of itself, but continuous operation in a rough regime is poor practice and makes for uncomfortable passengers.)

To set up best power, all that is necessary is to find peak EGT, then *enrichen* the mixture until EGT falls by100 to 125 degrees (four to five bars on the GEM). You can see from Fig. 2-1 that the "best power" point on the power curve corresponds to an EGT that is roughly 100 to 125 F rich of peak.

Setting up for best *economy* merely involves leaving the mixture at peak EGT, or up to 50 degrees (two bars) *lean* of peak. To wit: First find peak, then continue pulling the mixture control back until EGT drops 50 degrees (one or two bars on the Graphic Engine Monitor). This is where the specific fuel consumption curve in Fig. 2-1 "bottoms out," giving you the most miles per gallon for cruise.

Why don't peak EGT and best-power EGT coincide? After all, you'd think that the most efficient combustion (the point at which the fire burns hottest) would also give rise to the most power. The fact is that *gas expansion*, not heat *per se*, is what causes a piston to move and a crankshaft to turn. At fuel/air ratios slightly richer than stoichiometric, the maximum effective *gas pressure* is produced because more exhaust gas is evolved in combustion, due to the greater variety of incomplete-combustion byproducts produced. For example, more *carbon monoxide* molecules can be produced per molecule of oxygen than *carbon dioxide*, but since a gram of carbon monoxide takes up more space than a gram of carbon dioxide, the consequences for gas expansion—and piston movement—are enormous. Slightly rich F/A ratios favor the production of carbon monoxide (and other low-density, gaseous byproducts of incomplete combustion). This causes the *peak-pressure* F/A ratio to be somewhat greater than the *peak-temperature* F/A ratio. Hence, best *power* is reached 100 degrees or so on the rich side of peak EGT during the lean-out.

A technicality seldom mentioned in discussions of this sort is that merely because reactants are *present* in the combustion chamber in optimum chemical concentrations *doesn't necessarily mean* that they will burn completely. Researchers have measured the equilibrium concentrations of combustion products produced in stoichiometric combustion, at various temperatures and pressures, and they've found that both atomic oxygen (O) and molecular oxygen (O_2) are present in peak-EGT combustion gases. (At a combustion temperature of 3,100 degrees Fahrenheit and a pressure of 4 atm, O_2 is present at 0.1% concentration after "complete" burning of a stoichiometric iso-octane/air mixture. See *Internal Combustion Engine Fundamentals* by John Heywood, McGraw-Hill, 1988, pp. 432 and 830.) The fact that best-*power* mixture should fall on the rich side of stoichiometry is implicit in these observations, since unreacted oxygen equates to unused energy.

From a practical standpoint, it's worth noting that there are other methods, besides EGT, of identifying best-power mixture. In airplanes with fixed-pitch propellers, best-power can be attained by monitoring the tachometer and leaning to the point of maximum rpm. You can also attempt to set up best-power by reference to the airspeed indicator, since (obviously) airspeed increases with power. Unfortunately, however, *airspeed* increases *very slowly* with power—as the *cube* of horsepower, in fact—so that the relatively small increment of extra power obtainable by leaning (five to ten percent, depending on many factors) will barely register on the airspeed indicator of even a fast airplane. On a slow airplane, the increase in indicated airspeed may not even be perceptible.

The peak-EGT point on the curve can be thought of as the mixture that gives the most *total* heat from the combustion process, while the best-power point on the curve can be thought of as the mixture that gives the most *usable* heat (i.e., the most power). This is not necessarily the same thing, however, as getting *the most power per unit of fuel burned.* The best-power-per-unit-of-fuel point, or best-sfc point—frequently called the best-economy mixture—happens to occur at or near a fuel/air ratio of 0.059, or about 50 degrees F lean of peak-EGT. "But," you're probably saying, "you just got done telling me that you get the most *airspeed* over on the rich side of peak. How can you get better *mileage* at any other point on the graph than this?" The answer is that airspeed costs dearly in power, and power is paid for in fuel. If all you want is raw power, best-power mixture will give it to you, but you'll pay for it at the pump. If you want to minimize the *fuel-flow per horsepower* (i.e., maximize horsepower per gallon-per-hour), you should continue leaning past best-power. Surely, power will fall off as you continue pulling the mixture control back, but *so will fuel flow*—and since fuel flow falls off *faster* than power, you come out ahead. Eventually, if you continue leaning far enough, you'll reach a point where suddenly *power* begins to fall off faster than fuel flow. (In fact, your engine will eventually sputter and die—even though some fuel is still flowing.) That changeover point where the race between power-falloff and fuel-flow-falloff begins to be about equal is the region of best-economy—best horsepower per unit of fuel flow.

What happens to airspeed as you continue leaning from best-power to best-economy? And what happens to fuel consumption? The short answer is: The airspeed change is not dramatic, but the fuel-flow difference is attention-getting. According to the Cessna 182L operator's manual, leaning to a point 75 degrees on the rich side of peak—i.e., about midway between peak and best-power—will result in only a 1-mph loss of airspeed from best-power, but yields a net 10-percent increase in aircraft range. At peak EGT, the airspeed loss is about 3 mph compared to best-power; but the increase in range is now a full 20 percent! (Mind you, we're talking about a 20-percent increase in range compared to *best*-power mixture, not full rich mixture.)

Leaning to best-economy has a truly remarkable effect on range. Full-rich mixture is typically 50 percent overrich compared to best-power mixture; and best-power mixture is about 25 percent richer than best-economy. So the overall ratio of full-rich specific fuel consumption to best-economy specific fuel consumption is darn near two-to-one. An airplane that had a full-rich-mixture max range of 700 miles might thus go 900 miles when leaned to best-power, and perhaps 1,000 miles or more if leaned to best-economy.

How should you lean *your* engine? It depends. The choice of a mixture setting for cruise must be based on numerous factors, including the percentage power being used, the design and construction of the engine with respect to heat-sensitive parts (such as exhaust valves and turbochargers), the cooling efficiency of the particular airframe/engine installation, mixture maldistribution arising from poor induction system design, and—last but not least—the desire of the pilot to save fuel. (We'll have more to say about each of these matters in the next chapter.)

MIXTURE MALDISTRIBUTION

An extremely important practical consideration in the leaning of many aircraft engines is the phenomenon of mixture maldistribution. Getting exactly equal doses of fuel and air to each of an engine's four or six (or eight, or nine) cylinders is a far more difficult task than it first seems. Even in a fuel-injected engine (as we noted earlier), the individual cylinders are seldom operating at precisely the same F/A ratio. Fuel injector nozzles have a production tolerance (and get gummed up in service, if not cleaned often), and—more important—turbulence in the intake system, different-length induction pipes, gas-inertia effects, etc. combine to assure that not every cylinder gets the same exact amount of air, even with turbocharging. In fact, even in engines (such as the Piper Malibu's Continental TSIO-520-BE) that have been

The Piper Malibu's Continental TSIO-520-BE engine is one of few approved for continuous operation on the lean side of peak in high-power (80 percent) cruise. The ignition timing has been specially advanced and the induction system flow-tuned to allow this. As a rule, it is poor practice to operate on the lean side of peak (unless otherwise recommended by the engine or airframe manufacturer).

designed with a "tuned" induction system, one finds that optimum cylinder breathing only occurs within a very narrow rpm range; outside that range, unequal airflow again becomes a problem.

As you might expect, mixture maldistribution (variations in F/A ratio among the cylinders, at a given throttle setting an fuel-flow) shows up as EGT spread—i.e., the different cylinders will have different exhaust gas temperatures. Maldistribution is not the only contributor to inter-cylinder EGT spread, of course; we mentioned earlier that compression differences among cylinders can also result in uneven EGT indications. Factor compression differences and induction or fuel-flow peculiarities together, and you can come up with some pretty wild inter-cylinder EGT spreads, especially in carbureted engines, and especially at low power settings. (Even in a fuel-injected engine, a spread of 100 degrees between hottest and coldest cylinders is not unheard-of. It will vary with power setting and rpm.)

Why is mixture maldistribution an important consideration for leaning? Because the leanest cylinder(s) in an engine may start to cough and die—i.e., encounter so-called lean misfire—well before the richest cylinders reach best-economy EGT, or in some engines, even peak-EGT. Lean misfire has been explained (erroneously) as simple failure of combustion to occur when A/F ratios exceed 18:1. It is more correct to say that cyclic variations in charge strength, duration of combustion, and pressure-pulse timing *together* lead to increasing variability in the lean cylinder's power output. On some strokes, the cylinder is receiving a well-mixed, turbulent charge that burns quickly; on other strokes, the same cylinder is receiving poorly mixed fuel and air, which burns slowly and contributes little to engine power output. If you were to take a stroke-by-stroke movie of the lean cylinder in action, you would find that on some power strokes, combustion finishes early; on others, it finishes late. On some strokes, the cylinder may be making zero horsepower (or even *negative* power). In short, combustion doesn't *cease* at the lean limit; it just becomes more unpredictable. As John B. Heywood says (in *Internal Combustion Engine Fundamentals*, p. 427): "Too-slow flame development and propagation following successful ignition is usually the factor which limits engine operation with dilute mixtures."

When you progressively lean your engine to the point of roughness, you are merely causing some cylinders (the lean cylinders) to starve for fuel, and produce power unevenly, while the rest continue to run smoothly. In the real world, as a result, an engine with a relatively large EGT spread must, of necessity, be operated at overall richer mixtures than an engine with a small EGT spread. Why? Because the point of lean misfire (or more accurately, cycle-by-cycle combustion

Many engines, such as the Cessna 182's Continental O-470-R, encounter lean misfire at or before reaching peak EGT on the single-probe Cessna "economy mixture indicator." This is due to mixture maldistribution, which often can be ameliorated by application of partial carburetor heat, or simply changing the throttle setting slightly.

instability) is reached sooner with an engine that has one or more overlean cylinders. Leaning to peak EGT (overall, for the whole engine) might not even be possible; the lean jug may quit before you get there. This represents a serious limitation to the leaning of many engines. The Continental O-470-R used in the Cessna 182 is an example of an engine that exhibits a pronounced intercylinder EGT spread under cruise conditions (particularly in cold weather). Cessna's Pilot Operating Handbook for the 182L acknowledges this by stating that mixtures leaner than 25 degrees *rich* of peak may bring on lean misfire. (That's no misprint: Cessna said, and meant, *rich of peak*.)

Operators of carbureted aircraft should note that intercylinder EGT spread can often be reduced through judicious use of carburetor heat. Full carb heat has a fairly drastic effect on intake air temperatures (in fact, FAA certification rules require that the delta-T be at least 90 degrees), which in turn influences fuel vaporization. Tiny droplets of avgas that may not otherwise make it all the way to the farthest cylinders are better dispersed if they are vaporized first by heating. Try it yourself. Go up to normal cruise altitude, set the engine up for cruise, then—after smaking an initial (rough) mixture adjustment— slowly begin applying carburetor heat and note the effect on EGT spread. Experiment with varying amounts of carb heat to find the amount that works best. Then continue leaning. (You'll have to continue leaning anyway, since carb heat reduces the density of incoming air and effectively enrichens the mixture.)

Of course, bear in mind when using carburetor heat that opening the carb-heat valve admits unfiltered air to the engine intake system. Atmospheric dust—and dust from the inside of your engine compartment—will be free to enter the engine (and cause wear) any time carburetor heat is used.

Insight Instrument Corporation is typical in recommending that all leaning operations for cruise be conducted with reference to the leanest cylinder. This not only assures that lean misfire (combustion instability) is avoided during the normal cruise-leaning process, but also provides a margin of protection against detonation and overheating at advanced power settings. Leaning by reference to the leanest cylinder is standard operating procedure in most handbooks and provides the best assurance of safe, economical engine performance. (Leaning by reference to the *hottest* cylinder is less predictable, since *hotness* is a function of many things besides F/A ratio: for example, day-to-day variations in cylinder compression, variations in *total* fuel-and-air delivery to each cylinder, placement of the EGT probe in the exhaust pipe, etc.)

Unfortunately, many pilots (and one or two misinformed EGT manufacturers!) mistakenly equate "hottest cylinder" with "leanest cylinder." Occasionally an engine's hottest cylinder *is* the leanest cylinder, but this isn't always the case. *The leanest cylinder is the one that reaches peak EGT first as the mixture control is brought back.* It's hard to overemphasize the fact that *leanness is determined not on the basis of a static EGT reading, but by the dynamics of EGT variation.* Insight's Graphic Engine Monitor is the only EGT on the market that can find an engine's leanest cylinder automatically. The GEM does this not by reference to actual exhaust gas *temperature* but to comparative temperature trend information involving all of the engine's cylinders. Trend-comparison is the key to finding the leanest cylinder, whether visually or electronically. (Note, by the way, that the response rate of the EGT probe is not particularly crucial to one's ability to discern trend information; as long as all probes are identical in response, the actual response *rate* is of little importance. It's the comparative temperature *trend* you're interested in. Also, it's possible to guess the final temperature by watching the initial rate of change of the EGT indication. In mathematical terms, this is called looking at the first derivative of the temperature/time relationship. In the case of at least one EGT system—the Insight GEM—onboard software actually calculates temperature-curve derivatives to come up with a near-instantaneous prediction of final temperatures. This is a subtle, yet effective and accurate, way of getting around the age-old problem of "probe lag.")

Why is the hottest cylinder not necessarily the leanest? Consider what's required for combustion. It could be that your hottest cylinder is the one with the best compression—maybe all your other cylinders are comparatively leaky. Maybe your hottest cylinder is hottest simply because it's the jug getting the largest total amount of combustants (fuel-and-air). The more fuel, after all, the hotter the flame (if you have enough air to go with it, that is). It's even possible, if you think about it, for your *richest* cylinder to give the highest absolute EGT indication. The richest jug is merely the last one to peak; there's nothing preventing it from reaching the *highest* peak. Or the lowest peak. Or anything in between.

Again: The actual *magnitude* of your EGT indications is of little significance. You can't tell which jug is leanest simply by glancing at the panel instrument. Your leanest cylinder is the one that *reached peak EGT first* during leaning—not the one that happens to be hottest at the moment.

MATERIAL LIMITATIONS

For many engines, the main limitations to aggressive leaning are *material related*. That is to say, at the temperatures encountered in cruise at lean mixture settings, the material (strength and wear) properties of temperature-sensitive parts of the engine may be compromised unless limits are set on mixture strength and EGT.

It is a fact of life that the material properties of iron alloys deteriorate rapidly as temperatures increase beyond 1,000 degrees Fahrenheit. Not only do tensile strength and hardness go down (resulting in wear of moving parts), but corrosive attack—always a particular problem with components exposed to acid- and moisture-rich exhaust gases—increases dramatically, since corrosion is a chemical process and all chemical processes are logarithmically rate-related to temperature.

There's also the phenomenon known as "creep," which is the tendency of metal to become plastic and flow at high temperature. The creep limit of most austenitic (high-carbon) steels begins to be encountered at around 1,300 degrees Fahrenheit, increasing to about 1,700 degrees if high nickel content is specified.

Because of the unusual environment in which they operate, exhaust components—including exhaust valves, turbine housings, clamps, pipes, and EGT probes—are often coated with, or constructed wholly of, exotic metal alloys (known in the trade as superalloys). Mild steel might be acceptable for fabrication of an intake valve, since intake valves are cooled by a more-or-less continuous flow of fuel-and-air; but you won't find an aircraft-engine exhaust valve made of ordinary steel. The blowtorch effect of outrushing exhaust gases ensures that exhaust valves operate at or near the exhaust gas temperature itself. Special alloys are clearly called for.

Not only are special alloys called for in exhaust valves, but occasionally special design strategies, too, such as hollowing out the valve and filling it with elemental sodium. Sodium cooling of valves is a fairly old trick, dating to radial engine days. (Pilots can be justifiably proud of the fact that sodium-filled valves were actually first used in aircraft engines.) The idea is that the sodium—which melts at normal operating temperatures—sloshes back and forth inside the valve, carrying heat from the hottest part of the valve (namely the head) to the stem, where it can be dissipated across the relatively large area of the guide. If good guide contact is maintained, a sodium valve can operate as much as 200 degrees (F) cooler, at the head, than conventional solid-stemmed valves.

Current-production exhaust valves for Continental engines are solid-stemmed and fabricated from a special nickel alloy known as Nimonic 90. The stem is chrome-plated for hardness, the tip is specially case-hardened for good durability, and the face is coated with Stellite or nichrome alloy for corrosion resistance. Valve guides may be—in order of hardness—aluminum-bronze, cast-iron, or nitrided steel alloy ("nitralloy"). If you don't know which kind of guide your engine has, you should make an effort to find out. Bronzed guides have a characteristic bronze color when scraped lightly with a pocket knife. Continental IO-520, TSIO-520, and GTSIO-520 engines manufactured after 1981 have nitralloy guides. (The TSIO-360 and O-470 engines didn't get nitralloy until 1984.)

Current-production Lycoming exhaust valves, in contrast to Continental valves, are *sodium-filled* (which makes them quite a bit more expensive) and may or may not also employ exotic alloys, such as Inconel and Nimonic 80A. (Also, Lycoming valves may or may not be chromed on the stem, depending on part number.) As with Continental, Lycoming over the years has changed from softer to harder valve guides. Your Lycoming could contain aluminum-bronze or ni-resist (ductile iron) guides; the latter are now recommended for most applications. Again, you should make an effort to determine which kind of guide you have, since the high temperatures encountered with aggressive leaning have a detrimental effect on guide life (bronze especially).

The engine manufacturers' leaning recommendations are given in Teledyne Continental Service Bulletin M76-19, Revision 1, and Avco Lycoming Service Instruction No. 1094. For normally aspirated engines, Lycoming allows leaning to peak EGT at power settings up to 75 percent. (Above that, enrichen to full rich or as advised in the Pilot's Operating Handbook for the aircraft.) Continental, on the other hand, allows leaning to peak only for power settings up to 65 percent. For turbocharged engines, both manufacturers require that the turbine inlet temperature (TIT) be no higher than 1,650 Fahrenheit (with a couple of exceptions for a couple of engines).

Why not lean the engine to peak EGT at *all* powers? (Why have an

Turbocharged engines are subject to special restrictions for leaning, since it is easily possible to obtain TIT (turbine inlet temp) readings high enough to melt steel, simply by leaning to peak. A TIT redline of 1,650 Fahrenheit applies to most turbocharged models. The Cessna 402 shown here uses solid-stem-valve Continental TSIO-520-E engines, rated for 300-hp at 34.5 inches and 2,700 rpm.

upper limit of 75 or 65 percent at all?) Because at high power settings, leaning to peak can cause exhaust-valve overheating and attendant detonation. The detonation could, in theory, be combatted by using a higher-octane gasoline—but even with high-test fuel, you still wouldn't want to lean to peak above 75 percent power, because exhaust valve and cylinder head temperatures would be excessive. Early component wear (or failure) would be virtually guaranteed.

Why does Continental limit peak-EGT leaning to 65 percent while Lycoming chooses 75 percent? Probably because of differences in exhaust valve design. Continental's use of solid-stemmed valves puts an effective limit on how aggressively the mixture can be leaned before the valve overheats—the cooling margin afforded by sodium valves simply isn't there. Even with fairly conservative leaning, exhaust valve and guide wear can be a problem in high-output Continentals, particularly older models using bronze guides. TBOs (recommended time between overhauls) are uniformly lower for Continental engines than for Lycomings, probably again for this reason.

Am I going to tell you that your Continental engine will blow up if you lean it to peak EGT at power settings between 65 percent and 75 percent? No. Continental engines are certified to the same minimum detonation margins as Lycoming engines, and aggressive leaning will be no more hazardous with an O-200 than it would be with an O-235. In fact, peak-EGT operation will give longer spark-plug life in an O-200 operating at 75 percent power than will operating in accordance with Continental's bulletin. In higher-powered Continentals, peak-EGT operation at 75 percent power can lead to a trade-off between fuel economy and valve-guide life. (Many Continental IO-520 operators, acknowledging this, budget an extra two or three dollars an hour for top-overhaul work, and lean accordingly.) It's a question of horse-power versus fuel-flow versus temperature versus wear. There's no simple answer.

I wouldn't recommend that you lean a TSIO-520 or GTSIO-520 Continental to peak EGT at 75 percent, because detonation may occur if the compressor discharge temperature is high (as it will be at altitude), and TIT limits will be exceeded.

Use common sense where duty cycles and material limitations are concerned. A geared, turbocharged, solid-valved Continental GTSIO-520-L operating at 30 inches of manifold pressure in cruise is not going to tolerate the same degree of leaning, obviously, as a Lycoming O-360-A with sodium-cooled valves operating at cruise manifold pressures below 23 inches. In the former engine, the principal limitation to leaning is turbine inlet temperature (if not also detonation onset); a GTSIO-520 is capable of overheating exhaust valves and turbo housings in an instant. With the O-360, the main limitation to leaning will be the onset of lean misfire; under normal circumstances (i.e., cruise powers below 75 percent), valve overheating and detonation are not limiting in this engine.

SPECIAL CONSIDERATIONS
FOR TURBOCHARGED ENGINES

All of the above consideration apply to turbocharged engines, but in addition, a few special considerations apply. By virtue of their duty cycle, turbocharged powerplants operate closer to cylinder-cooling limits, detonation limits, and material limits (for valve guides, pistons, valves, turbo housings, etc.) than other engines. These factors must be weighed when deciding on a mixture-management protocol for a turbocharged engine.

The principal limitation for leaning a T-engine (TO-, TIO-, TIGO-,

TSIO-, or GTSIO-, etc.), assuming CHT is not a problem, is TIT—turbine inlet temperature. Turbine housings, commonly made either of 321 stainless or D2 Ni-resist (ductile cast-iron), are prone to creep problems and thermal stress relief problems (i.e., cracking) if TIT is allowed to go too high.

How high is high? Most T-series powerplants have an arbitrary TIT redline of 1,650 degrees Fahrenheit, continuous. (Some handbooks allow leaning to TITs of 1,700 degrees or more for brief periods, for the purpose of finding peak EGT. Consult your POH or engine operating guide.) A conservative approach would be to keep TIT below 1,600 continuous, with only occasional forays into the

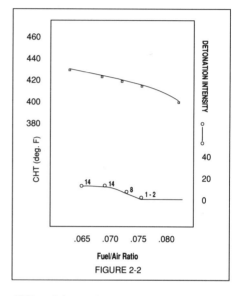

FIGURE 2-2

CHT and detonation intensity versus mixture strength for a Lycoming TIO-540-J2BD engine operating at economy cruise power at 18,000 feet (after Sibole, SAE 790630). CHT is plotted in the upper half of the graph; detonation intensity is plotted in the lower half as "flashes per minute" on a Sperry Engine Analyzer oscilloscope screen. Trace detonation occurs at a fuel/air ratio of .076, corresponding to best-power mixture. Further leaning causes a mild increase in detonation.

1,650 area to find peak-EGT. Any lowering of continuous operating temperatures will bring with it a worthwhile salutary effect on turbocharger and wastegate life, particularly with Rajay turbochargers, where aluminum bearing housings are used.

At high cruising altitudes, cylinder head temperatures can approach redline in many turbocharged aircraft, requiring the use of richer mixtures and/or opened cowl flaps. (Because of density effects, ram-air cooling is actually worse at high altitude than down low, even though outside air temperatures are frigid.) CHT responds more slowly than EGT or TIT, but it should be monitored closely in a turbocharged aircraft during climbing and cruising flight, and appropriate mixture adjustments made to keep CHT in check. It is interesting to note that in the days of the large piston-powered airliners (before widespread use of EGT or TIT), the highly supercharged engines were often leaned entirely by reference to CHT.

Detonation limits are much slimmer for a turbocharged engine operating at high pressure ratio (i.e., wastegate closed) than for a comparable normally aspirated engine, due to the fact that the turbo-compressed intake air is often quite hot when it arrives at the cylinder. (The effect is not unlike operating with fulltime carburetor heat.)

Fig. 2-2 shows a plot of detonation intensity versus fuel/air ratio for a Lycoming TIO-540-J2BD operating at approximately 55 percent power at 18,000 feet.

Detonation onset is encountered at a F/A ratio of .076, which corresponds to best-power mixture. Leaning to peak produces potentially damaging levels of detonation. (Paradoxically, the Lycoming operator's manual for this engine permits leaning to best economy at the power setting shown.)

The same engine, operated at 55 percent *at* sea level, probably would not detonate as readily, due to the fact that the turbocharger is not working as hard down low.

In Fig. 2-2, the engine is operating at a manifold pressure of 35 inches (redline for this engine is 46 inches), but the ambient air pressure at 18,000 feet is 15 inches. The turbo compressor is thus operating at a pressure ratio of 35 divided by 15, or 2.3 (minimum).

Deck air temperature is a function of pressure ratio and compressor efficiency. Under the conditions specified in Fig. 2-2, the compressor discharge air temperature would be on the order

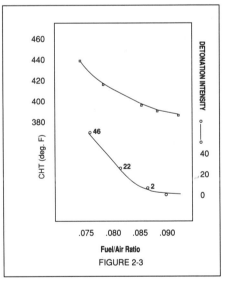

FIGURE 2-3

CHT and detonation intensity versus mixture strength for a Lycoming TIO-540-J2BD operating at 40 inches and 2,400 rpm (performance cruise power) at 18,700 feet simulated pressure altitude. (Fuel: Exxon 100LL.) Detonation begins at F/A ratios well on the rich side of best-power and increases in severity rapidly as best-power EGT is approached. (Compare with Fig. 2-2.) Note the steep rise in CHT as well.

of 263 degrees Fahrenheit. (At sea level, the deck air would be about 100 degrees, at the same manifold pressure.)

Figure 2-3 (which, like Figure 2-2, is adapted from John Sibole, Jr., SAE 790630) shows detonation characteristics of the TIO-540-J2BD engine at "performance cruise" power (40 in. MP and 2,400 rpm) at 18,700 feet simulated pressure altitude. Notice that significant detonation is encountered well below best-power F/A ratios (.076-.082). The induction air temperature for this run was only 31 to 34 degrees Fahrenheit. Nevertheless, by the time the intake air comes out the downwind side of the turbo compressor, it is hot enough to cause detonation at relatively rich F/A ratios.

The purpose of this discussion is not to make you an expert on detonation, but to give you an idea of the factors at work in a turbocharged engine and the many considerations that must be born in mind when deciding on a "best" mixture for a turbocharged engine. Leaning an aircraft engine—any aircraft engine—is not something to be approached haphazardly or in an ill-informed manner, but that applies double when it comes to leaning a *turbocharged* engine.

MIXTURE MANAGEMENT
BY PHASE OF FLIGHT

Pilots have traditionally been taught to lean their engines only in cruise flight, and generally only above 5,000 feet. At all other times, according to tradition, an airplane's engine should not be leaned at all unless it is stumbling due to overrichness from high density altitude.

With the advent of the EGT (the GEM in particular)—and with avgas becoming increasingly costly—it is no longer necessary or economically appropriate to adhere to the familiar bromides of a bygone era when it comes to leaning. By paying proper attention to the engine's true mixture needs, an engine can and should be leaned for regimes of flight other than cruise. If you lean *only* in cruise, you can expect rapid spark plug fouling, high fuel bills, and generally increased maintenance costs (to say nothing of reduced aircraft performance).

An engine's mixture requirements vary with the phase of flight. This fact is reflected in the *mixture schedule* designed into the carburetor or fuel injector system, as shown in Fig. 2-4. Offhand, one might assume that at full throttle (when the demand for power is high), an engine's carburetor should be set to give best-power mixture, while at reduced throttle settings an appropriate mixture, generally speaking, might be a best-economy setting, or perhaps a stoichiometric mixture. But we see from Fig. 2-4 (which shows the fuel/air ratio of a Continental IO-520 at full rich mixture over a wide range of throttle settings) that the actual "designed in" mixture schedule deemed appropriate by factory engineers differs markedly from the "ideal" mixture schedule we have postulated. Not only is the mixture far to the rich side of stoichiometric, but it is actually richer than best-power at all power settings. And it varies with respect to power setting.

Why does Fig. 2-4 look the way it does? The rich fuel/air ratio at high power settings is needed for cylinder cooling and detonation suppression. (Current FAA certification standards call for a 12 percent mixture margin against detonation at full power. That is, the pilot must be able to reduce fuel flow by 12 percent at wide-open throttle and not encounter detonation on takeoff at sea level.) Super-richness at idle is necessary for smooth engine response when the throttle is opened. (Sudden throttle opening causes a quick inrush of air to the engine which, if not counteracted with a corresponding extra brief rush of fuel, results in the engine stumbling while it picks up speed.) To some extent, overrichness is needed at power settings *above* idle as

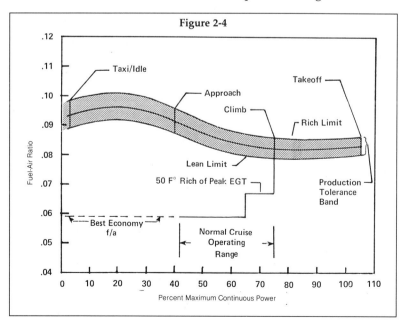

Figure 2-4

Leaning on takeoff is not only permissible but highly advisable when density altitude is more than 5,000 feet, as it often is in the desert southwest. Lean for maximum rpm or manifold pressure, or as directed in the operating handbook for the airplane or engine.

well, for good transient throttle response. But on top of all this, an extra bit of enrichening must be included to accommodate fuel-system insensitivity to adverse changes in ambient pressure and temperature. And finally, some additional overrichness must be designed into the schedule to provide for production tolerances on fuel injector systems (and carburetors). The result: One whale of a rich engine, except under worst-case full-throttle conditions.

Obviously, for engine startup it is advisable to have the mixture control in the full rich position, to assure adequate fuel for combustion. But once the engine is idling, it can be leaned. In fact, as Fig. 2-4 suggests, it can be leaned to a remarkable degree before lean misfire is encountered. Can you *hurt* your engine by leaning it at idle? Definitely not. Temperatures inside the cylinders (and at the spark plug tips) are low; leaning can only make the engine run smoother and the plugs burn cleaner. Before opening the throttle, of course, the mixture should be enriched as necessary to allow smooth engine acceleration. While taxiing, however, the mixture can be left leaned.

Leaning during the takeoff roll is not something most pilots are accustomed to doing, even on hot/high takeoffs. If done with care, however, takeoff leaning can provide an extra measure of engine performance and fuel economy for departures not involving "standard day" or below-sea-level density altitude conditions. (Takeoff leaning is *not* recommended for turbocharged engines; consult your operator's handbook or flight manual for the manufacturer's recommended procedures.) On aircraft equipped with appropriate fuel-flow instrumentation, the full-power altitude reference markings indicate desirable fuel flows for various altitudes (typically S.L., 3,000, 5,000, 7,000, etc.), whereas some aircraft are allowed a specified exhaust-gas temperature (e.g., 150 deg. rich of peak) as the allowable takeoff power mixture.

In the climb, most normally aspirated aircraft will experience less plug fouling, better engine performance, smoother operation, and enhanced operating economy if the engine is leaned. Remember, the full-rich mixture setting is designed to provide maximal fuel cooling for *sea-level takeoff*. As the aircraft climbs, air density decreases by approximately three percent per thousand feet of elevation. You are therefore justified in leaning the engine a couple of percent per thousand feet during the ascent. If you don't, the mixture will become about three percent richer per thousand feet—as indicated by a *drop* in overall EGT. A conservative procedure would be to take off full rich at sea level, wait until a drop in EGT is noted during the climb, and begin leaning as necessary to restore the sea-level (or takeoff elevation) EGT indication. This will assure adequate fuel flow with minimum plug fouling and good engine performance.

Notwithstanding this advice, the pilot should check the approved flight manual for the aircraft to ensure that manufacturer's limitations for leaning in climb are adhered to. In many aircraft equipped with fuel-flow gauges, the FF gauge face has blue "climb" markings to indicate appropriate fuel-flow for climb. With turbocharged aircraft in particular, the manufacturer's climb-leaning limitations should be closely followed.

How the engine is leaned during cruise will depend (as stated further above) on many factors, including the engine's cooling needs (as determined by CHT indications), the need to increase range or endurance, the operator's desire to make TBO without a top overhaul, etc. Where high power, long engine life, good cooling, and good detonation margins are considerations, operation on the rich side of peak will be desirable.

Where good spark plug life and improved fuel economy are prime considerations, it may be advisable to lean to peak (if the engine is below 75 percent power, and mixture maldistribution is not severe). Where range and/or endurance are critical, operation on the lean side

Traffic-pattern leaning, practiced by many trainer operators to prevent plug fouling, is not harmful to the engine since the power setting is well below 75 percent (on downwind, base, and final). Students should be cautioned to return the mixture to full-rich before turning final, or any time a go-around is imminent.

of peak EGT should be considered (again if mixture maldistribution doesn't present a problem).

Keeping the mixture leaned during the descent will generally extend spark plug life, keep CHTs in the proper range, and allow smooth engine operation; there is certainly no *a priori* reason why the mixture should suddenly be moved to full-rich at the beginning of a letdown. (In fact, if carburetor heat is applied for the descent, the mixture should be *re-leaned* to an appropriate EGT indication—e.g., peak EGT—since it will otherwise be shifted rich.) Some enrichening of the mixture is advisable as denser air is encountered at lower altitudes, particularly if the power setting is high. During low-power letdowns, however, leaning to peak is a sound procedure.

Leaning in the traffic pattern will also pay dividends in terms of fuel economy and spark plug reliability, but it is important to remember the effect of leaning on transient throttle response. If a go-around (or major application of power) is anticipated, the mixture should be enrichened generously prior to throttle opening. "Enrichened generously" doesn't always mean full rich, however. If you are landing at Denver, Colorado, leaning all the way to touchdown is a perfectly good idea.

With experience, the careful operator can apply the principles of mixture management to all phases of operation, with potentially spectacular improvements in operating economy and engine performance. When in doubt, however, consult the aircraft or engine manufacturer's handbook. Remember that *improper* leaning has an even more spectacular *negative* payoff, in terms of possible engine damage and associated costs (as we'll see in Chapter Five).

Chapter 3

CRUISE-LEANING SETPOINTS

So much misinformation has been propagated over the years (chiefly by flight instructors and lounge hounds; occasionally by the manufacturers themselves) on the subjects of peak EGT, best economy EGT, best power, finding the "leanest cylinder," etc., that it's only reasonable to include a short review of the major EGT setpoints, and their implications for leaning, here. (For a longer discussion of the combustion dynamics involved, see Chapter Two.) More than one mechanic has commented, in the course of a top overhaul, "See here? The guy bought one of those fancy 'exhaust analyzers,' then went out and burned up his engine!" Unfortunately, there's a good deal of truth in this comment. Pilots do, as a rule, tend to gain a false sense of confidence from the digital accuracy afforded by the latest crop of EGT/TIT engine monitoring systems, and those pilots who lack a thorough understanding of the combustion process *as it applies to their*

engine often end up buying premature top overhauls. When it comes to understanding EGT, a little knowledge can indeed be dangerous.

The first thing to realize (as simple as it sounds) is that metal will melt at high temperature, and exhaust systems are made of metal. Actually, of course, metals have the interesting property of becoming *plastic* (capable of stretching or flowing) well before they melt, at high temperatures. This property is called "creep." For austenitic (high-carbon) steels, creep begins at something like 1,200 or 1,300 degrees Fahrenheit (it varies by alloy)—a temperature easily attainable in any airplane engine's exhaust system. C.F. Taylor, writing in *The Internal Combustion Engine in Theory and Practice, Vol. II,* puts the temperature "above which endurance limit is adversely affected" at 660 deg. F for low-carbon steel, 800 F for medium-carbon steel, 930 F for austenitic steel, and 1,380 F for Nimonic alloy. (These values are all on the low side, but instructive nonetheless.) Fortunately, exhaust valves for current-production Continental engines are made wholly of Nimonic alloy; Lycoming uses Nimonics as well as Inconel. Still, even these special superalloys (which contain almost no iron; the chief constituent being nickel) will creep and flow (not to mention erode, in the presence of exhaust gas) at temperatures above 1,600 F. Absolute temperature thus becomes a leaning criterion, if engine (and exhaust system) TBO is to be preserved. Many aircraft engines are incapable of producing EGT indications of 1,600 or more, *but many can.* If your engine is one of those that is capable of generating EGT or TIT indications in the 1,600-or-above region, limit your leaning so as never to go above 1,600 or 1,650 F, max-continuous, regardless of where that puts you in terms of best-power, best-economy, or other setpoints. (The choice of 1,650 as TIT redline by the engine manufacturers is essentially arbitrary. Remember that the indicated TIT will vary depending on where the probe is placed.) Never exceed 1,650 F during leaning (except for brief periods, to find peak).

A second major limitation on leaning is detonation (see Chapter 5). Detonation margins vary significantly from engine model to engine model (and from day to day, as cylinder compression and OAT change). In general, if you avoid leaning to peak EGT at power settings higher than 65%, you'll be detonation-free on 100LL avgas no matter what type of engine(s) you're flying behind (assuming, of course, there is nothing mechanically wrong with the engine, and the mag timing is on-spec). As the percent of rated power increases, however, your margin of protection against detonation at peak EGT dwindles.

Since there is no easy, foolproof way to detect detonation from the cockpit, one must be a bit conservative in choosing one's leaning guidelines; this is why, for example, most leaning is done by reference to the *leanest cylinder*.

Different rules apply to different engines, depending on such things as design compression ratio and the presence or absence of turbocharging. Common sense says that if you're flying a low-compression, 80-octane engine (such as a Lycoming O-320-E2D or Continental O-470-R) on 100LL avgas, your knock-limited "percent power" is going to be much higher than if you are flying a high-compression engine with turbocharging (e.g., a pair of Rajayed 8.7:1 Lycoming IO-540s in an Aerostar 601). In the latter case, you probably wouldn't want to lean to peak EGT at anything above 55% power; and even then, you'd want to monitor EGT and CHT for your leanest cylinder(s) carefully.

Hard-and-fast rules simply do not apply. Each aircraft owner must decide for himself or herself which leaning regimens are best for his/her own airplane, under a particular set of conditions.

With this in mind, let's look quickly at the pros and cons of various popular leaning setpoints, starting with the richest and most conservative.

BEST-POWER MIXTURE
(125 F on the Rich Side of Peak)

Best-power mixture is a very conservative leaning setpoint, not only because it is cool enough (compared to peak EGT) to keep exhaust-valve thermal erosion and creep to a minimum, but because there is enough extra fuel in the mixture to allow significant extra cylinder and valve cooling (with the attendant detonation protection). Best-power leaning also offers the attractive bonus of providing maximum aircraft performance: airspeed is maximum, cooling inflow through the cowl is maximum, rate-of-climb (should it be needed) is maximum, and time getting to one's destination will be minimum, compared to any other mixture setting (for a given manifold pressure and rpm). Since hydrocarbons are present in excess, carbon buildup will be slightly higher at this mixture setting (over the long haul) than at peak EGT, but the effect is not substantial, since scavenging is also good at best-power mixture. Overall, because of the extra cooling afforded by the added fuel flow (vis-a-vis peak EGT), TBO prospects are probably better for best-power mixture than for any other mixture setpoint. This is certainly true for turbocharged engines, whic need not only the cooling but the detonation margin afforded by this setting.

Bear in mind that best-power mixture results in an overall increase in engine power of five percent or more, compared to full-rich mixture. (At very high altitudes, where the engine will not run smoothly at full-rich mixture, the power gain can be much more than 5% when leaning to best-power.) So before leaning, set your throttle and prop controls to give a "percent power" figure a few percent shy of your desired final power. Then lean to best-power mixture. Otherwise—if you start full rich, and set up 75% power on the MP and tach—it is possible that you will end up at 80% power (or more) after leaning, without knowing it. (The relationship of EGT and engine power to F/A ratio is depicted in Fig. 3-1.)

Eligible engines: All models (provided the power setting is 75% or less). Turbocharged engines such as Continental's TSIO-360, TSIO-470, TSIO-520, and GTSIO-520 series, and Lycoming's TO-360, TIO-

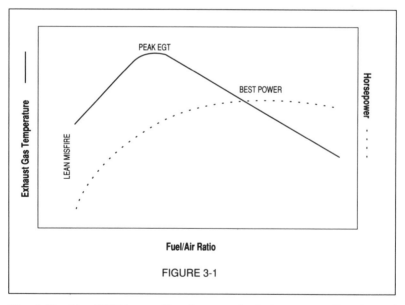

FIGURE 3-1

The relationship of EGT to overall engine power (and mixture strength) is depicted qualitatively by this graph. Best power occurs at a mixture well to the rich side of peak EGT, and results in approximately five percent more horsepower than full rich (at altitudes below 10,000 feet). Best-power mixture gives best cruise speed, and is fairly conservative, tending to protect the engine from top-end damage.

540, and TIO-541 series, probably should be leaned no leaner than best-power in high cruise.

Not recommended for: Best-power mixture is not recommended for power settings above 75%, regardless of engine make/model; also, engines that approach 1,650 F for EGT or TIT during best-power leaning probably should be allowed to run richer than best power.

PEAK EGT

Peak EGT occurs when air and fuel are present in precisely the correct chemical balance (the so-called stoichiometric ratio). The greatest heat release occurs at this mixture setting, and as a result CHT is prone to be high (although theoretically, CHT peaks at a fuel/air ratio slightly rich of max-EGT). The power delivered to the crankshaft is less than at peak-power EGT (above), because the amount of gas evolved in combustion is less and combustion is shifted late. (Maximum flame velocity occurs at a mixture richer than stoichiometric, around 1.2 equivalence ratio or F/A = .080.) The chief advantage of operating at peak EGT is increased fuel economy. Specific fuel consumption (lbs/hr/hp) at peak EGT is on the order of 20% lower than at best-power mixture. Airspeed is also degraded, however, since the engine is developing less power. A secondary benefit of peak-EGT combustion is that it leaves very few combustion byproducts (i.e., deposits). The oil remains uncontaminated for a longer period (providing blowby is minimal to begin with) and the combustion chamber—including the spark plugs—will tend to stay cleaner, longer.

Unfortunately, exhaust-system temperatures as a whole are high, and detonation protection at its lowest, at peak EGT. Both factors can be important for high-output engines. The impact on TBO is nil to seriously negative, depending on how hot the engine runs.

In some engines, such as the O-470-R, it may not be possible to operate smoothly at peak EGT (when EGT is measured from a single probe that averages one bank of cylinders), since mixture maldistribution can cause lean misfire to appear in the leanest cylinders before peak EGT for the engine-as-a-whole has been reached.

Eligible engines: Good candidates for peak-EGT leaning include the Lycoming O-235-C, E, K, L, N; the O-320 series (except O-320-H, which deserves to be a bit on the rich side of peak except at 60% and below); IO-320-E and AEIO-320-E; O-360-B & D; GO-480 series except -G models; and O-540-B series. Others can be leaned to peak as well, but power settings should be adjusted to 60% or below. Continental engines: A-series, C-series, and O-200; O-300-D; E-series and low-compression O-470 (i.e., all except O-470-U); normally aspirated IO-series engines operating well away from 75% power; TSIO-520-B at 55% or less; TSIO-520-AE and -BE; intercooled TSIO-series engines operating well away from 75%.

Not recommended for: TO-360, TIO-360, GO-480-G, GSO- and IGSO-series, TIO-540, TIO-541, TIGO-541, helicopter engines (Lycoming); IO-360 series, TSIO-360 series, O-470-U, non-intercooled TSIO-520, GTSIO-520 (Continental). Rajay-retrofitted engines, unless wastegate is open.

BEST-ECONOMY MIXTURE
(50 F on the Lean Side of Peak)

Best-economy mixture can be defined as *that mixture setting which gives the lowest possible specific fuel consumption for a given manifold pressure and rpm.* Where does "best economy" mixture occur relative to EGT? Some say "at peak EGT"; others say "just slightly on the lean side of peak." The truth is that for a well-tuned engine in which all jugs run at the same F/A ratio, best economy comes on the lean side of peak, at a fuel/air ratio of about 0.059, not *at* peak. That's because although fuel flow and horsepower both decrease with continued leaning beyond peak, fuel flow actually falls off *faster* than engine power (initially, at least). After a certain point, power begins to fall off faster than fuel flow (due to cycle-by-cycle and cylinder-by-cylinder variations in burn rate and mixture strength) and continued leaning only causes the engine to stumble and die.

Where some cylinders run rich and some run lean (which is certainly the case in a great many engines), complications arise, because in looking at the engine's overall sfc, one is actually looking at the *average* of the individual cylinder sfcs. And since an engine's leanest cylinders may begin to misfire before the richer ones have reached *peak* EGT, best-economy mixture *for the engine as a whole* is often biased toward the rich side of the EGT curve. In other words, best economy may come at peak EGT, or even slightly on the *rich* side of peak EGT, for a poorly tuned engine with just one TIT or EGT probe (situated in a downstream location).

Compression ratio is also important. It turns out that the higher the compression ratio, the faster the burn rate; and the faster the burn rate, the further on the lean side of peak you can go before engine power output begins to fall off. This has to do with the fact that charge mixing and swirl factors tend to be higher (leading to faster combustion) in a high-compression engine. Lean mixtures burn slower and tend to delay peak combustion pressures to later in the Otto cycle, where the piston tends to have less mechanical advantage over the crank. In a high-compression engine, peak combustion pressure is reached earlier in the cycle, and the power-robbing effects of ultra-lean mixtures are forestalled. (See Fig. 3-2.)

What it all means is, you shouldn't expect a Continental C-75, with a compression ratio of 6.5:1, to exhibit the same "best economy" leaning behavior (relative to EGT) as a Lycoming O-360-E with a C.R. of 9.0:1. A high-compression engine is going to tolerate leaning much further on the lean side of peak than a low-compression engine, before reaching "best economy mixture" (assuming mixture maldistribution doesn't moot the argument). Bear in mind, though, that when one

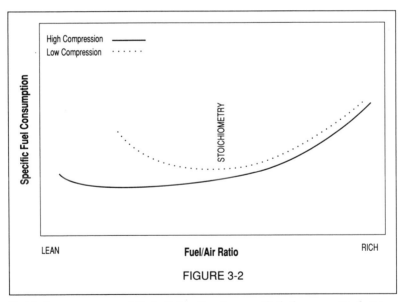

FIGURE 3-2

Best fuel economy occurs at the fuel/air ratio where specific fuel consumption bottoms (by definition). For many engines, sfc bottoms at or near the stoichiometric mixture point, otherwise known as peak EGT. For certain high-compression and/or fast-burn engine types, the sfc curve actually bottoms well on the lean side of peak EGT or stoichiometry. Obviously, since each individual cylinder has its own particular compression efficiency (depending on valve and ring sealing at the time of measurement), the shape and positioning of the sfc curve varies from cylinder to cylinder even within a given engine. (After Heywood, 1988.)

The Cessna 152's Lycoming O-235-L2C (and the 150's O-200-A) can and should be leaned more aggressively than a high-performance engine. Leaning to peak EGT—or even the point of roughness—can extend spark plug life, conserve fuel, and contribute to lower life-cycle operating costs.

cylinder is running so much richer or leaner than another that your inter-cylinder EGT spread is 150 or 200 degrees Fahrenheit, it's difficult to say with precision exactly where best-economy mixture is going to fall. Often, you're best off just leaning to peak on the leanest cylinder (or leaning to the point of misfire, then enrichening slightly, if you don't have a multiprobe system), and calling *that* "best economy."

The advantages of running on the lean side of peak are low temperatures (relative to peak), low fuel consumption, and better range and endurance (which can be important in a low-fuel emergency). The low-temperature advantage is probably a worthless one, however, since oxidative attack of exhaust components is sharply increased by operation on the lean (oxygen-rich) side of peak; also, very little cooling effect is coming from the fuel itself, so CHT does not respond in quite the way you'd expect.

The disadvantages of "best economy" operation include greatly reduced aircraft performance (airspeed may be off as much as 5 or 10 mph from best-power mixture), rough engine operation (in many cases), and shortened TBO due to oxidative attack of exhaust and combustion chamber components.

Eligibile engines: Lycoming O-235-C, E, H; O-320-A, C, E; O-540-B. Continental A-65, A-75, C-75, C-85, C-90, O-200-A, O-300-D, IO-360 series (65% or less). Continental also advises (in fact, demands) TSIO-520-BE operators run at best-economy mixtures, although this procedure has brought controversial results. High-compression engine models may be leaned to best economy at power settings of 65% or less, consistent with manufacturers' recommendations and lean misfire limits.

Not recommended for: Continental TSIO-360 series, O-470, IO-470, TSIO-520 series (except -BE), GTSIO-520; Lycoming O-235-F, O-320-H, O-360-E, TO-series, and TIO-540 series engines.

Once again, note that nothing in this chapter is meant to supersede engine or airframe manufacturers' recommendations. If you elect to depart from manufacturers' recommendations, you do so at your own risk.

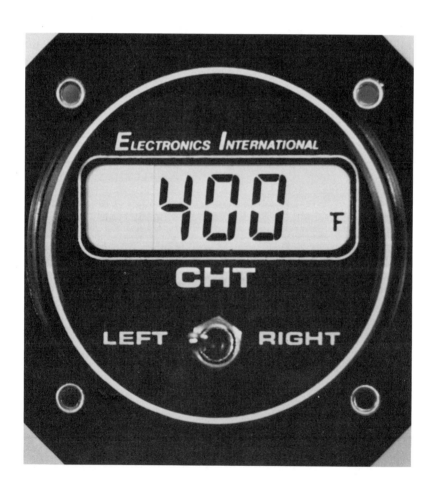

Chapter 4

CYLINDER HEAD TEMPERATURE (CHT)

Cylinder head temperature instrumentation is among the oldest forms of aircraft engine "condition monitoring" and in an air-cooled engine assumes more than passing significance since overheating is an ever-present (and potentially quite expensive) possibility. CHT monitoring depends on the use of individual probes at the cylinders which provide electrical signals that are converted into some form of temperature readout (on the GEM, a non-illuminated "black bar" in the field of orange EGT bars). Pilots are accustomed to thinking of CHT as a slow-to-change phenomenon—and it is. The slow response of CHT to power changes, airspeed changes, etc., has little to do with the response characteristics of the CHT probe, however; the probe's response time is much faster than it needs to be. Rather, it's the *cylinder* head that changes temperature slowly, because of its huge mass.

CHT is an important adjunct to exhaust analysis (as we saw in the previous chapter). Its indications can often be correlated with EGT readouts to arrive at a better understanding of the combustion process, be it normal or abnormal. The main significance of CHT to the pilot, however, when it comes to normal flight (normal engine operation) is twofold: First and foremost, the pilot is interested in preventing cylinder head overheating, or overtemping. (When cylinder head temperatures are high, material properties of aluminum heads, valves, guides, pistons, etc. are seriously degraded, and engine life is shortened accordingly.) Secondly, the pilot is interested in preventing *shock cooling* of the cylinders.

Shock cooling has been the subject of some debate in recent years, with some people suggesting that it may be a figment of the engineer's imagination. Any overhauler who routinely works on engines from skydiving jump planes, banner tow planes, glider tugs, etc., will attest to the existence of shock cooling, however. Rapid cooling of a hot metallic object causes it to change dimension. (It shrinks.) With cylinder heads, the problem arises that not all of the constituent components of the head assembly are made of the same alloy, and different alloys shrink at different rates (and to different final sizes) with rapid cooling. Valve seats, for example, are made of hardened steel and pressed (interference-fitted) into aluminum cylinder heads. Since aluminum's coefficient of thermal expansion is about double that of steel, the valve seat is "pinched" rather tightly during rapid cylinder cooldown. The aluminum around the seat has nowhere to go, however, so stress buildups occur in areas immediately adjacent to the valve seat. With successive rapid heatup/cooldown cycles, spontaneous stress relief of the head in these areas is a distinct possibility. And indeed, cylinder head cracks running from valve seat to valve seat are common.

The principal harmful effect of shock cooling is thus internal cylinder-head cracking. Typical crack-formation areas include not only the areas surrounding valve seats and spark plug holes, but also the areas surrounding valve guides, injector nozzles, and head-to-barrel joints. Cracking can also occur anywhere that tool marks, sharp edges, and other "stress risers" may be found.

Cracking is not the only form of shock-cooling damage, however. Sudden changes in valve temperature have been known to warp valves (and seats), causing poor valve sealing and compression loss. In addition, there is considerable evidence (not only from owner reports, but from controlled testing) that valve sticking can occur as the guide shrinks faster than the hot valve on the cooldown cycle. According to Lycoming's Ken Johnson, writing in the Avco Lycoming *Flyer* (May 1982): "Engineering tests have demonstrated that valves will stick when a large amount of very cold air is directed over an engine which has been quickly throttled back after operating at normal running temperatures."

Of course, when a valve sticks in anything but the full-open position, the pushrod, lifter, and rocker jam up under pressure from the camshaft lobe(s). Something's got to give. Generally, it's the pushrod (which takes a permanent bend), although also rocker bosses have been known to crack, lifters collapse, cam lobes scuff and spall, etc. When valves stick in the *open* position, these factors are not important; what's important is that the protruding valve can (and will) contact the piston dome on the piston's next up-cycle, resulting in very costly damage not only to the piston and valve, but (if the valve breaks, and it's a turbocharged engine) the downstream exhaust components, turbine wheels in particular. (We are aware of cases, also, where busted-off valve pieces have been sucked back out the intake valve and "redistributed" to other cylinders, causing damage throughout the engine.)

In SAE Technical Paper No. 790605 (Society of Automotive Engineers, 1979), Continental engineers Bernard Rezy, Kenneth Stuckas, Jay Meyers, and J. Ronald Tucker make the following observations: "[Something that is] difficult to quantify is the reduction in cylinder head durability due to low cycle thermal stress superimposed upon the high cycle mechanical stress of combustion pressure. This low cycle thermal stress is caused by the

KS Avionics makes a variety of CHT and EGT/CHT combination gauges with CHT overtemp and shock-cooling annunciation. The overtemp and shock-cooling annunciation thresholds can be user-set to any desired value. KSA suggests a ballpark figure of one-degree-F-per-second as being a suitable threshold for shock-cooling purposes.

normal aircraft operating cycle—high cylinder head temperatures during takeoff and climb modes of operation and low temperatures during high-speed descent modes. Leaning to best-economy in descent at low powers results in cylinder head temperatures which are lower than at best-power or even full-rich fuel flow. This overcooling effect can have an impact on cylinder head life."

The foregoing paragraph contains many interesting observations. We see, among other things, one immediate clue to avoiding shock-cooling damage: I.e., do not descend with the mixture leaned to best-economy at low power. Keep some power on the engine and/or relean to keep EGTs near cruise values, so as to maintain a healthy CHT, or a healthy *rate* of CHT decrease.

Neither the airframe manufacturers nor the engine manufacturers specify an appropriate cooloff *rate* for cylinder heads, so it is difficult to know where the "safe" limits are. Mooney recommends a descent profile for the 231 that results in an approximate 30-degree-per-minute cooldown rate in the descent, and this would certainly seem to be a conservative procedure. (On the Insight GEM, look for a one-bar CHT change every 60 to 90 seconds during letdown, and if the cooloff rate becomes too fast, modulate power, airspeed, cowl flaps, rpm, mixture, etc. accordingly.)

Monitoring shock-cooling is something that is difficult to do with meaningful regularity in the absence of multiprobe CHT instrumentation. Original equipment CHT installations offer extremely limited CHT information, owing to the fact that only one probe is used, and that probe is often located only on the hottest cylinder (or at least, the cylinder location that was hottest on the factory test airplane which determined the type design). Federal Aviation Regulations require that

A numeric representation of CHT indications is popular (and appropriate), since CHT data is slow to change, and since most pilots monitor only one cylinder for CHT anyway. This Electronics International gauge incorporates three-way monitoring for EGT (one probe), CHT, and oil temperature.

airframe manufacturers locate the CHT probe on the hottest cylinder in climb, as determined by flight testing. This location can vary even within a given airplane model run, depending on location of cooling baffles, engine accessories, exhaust system design, etc., from year to year. The cylinder that the factory probe is installed on is apt to be warm-indicating all the time, relative to the other cylinders. You have no idea what your *other* jugs are doing, unless you have installed a full Graphic Engine Monitor system, or other aftermarket multiprobe system.

Regardless of the letdown regimen you decide on, one thing is clear. "It is poor technique to 'chop' the power from cruise or higher settings to idle and then start a rapid letdown which develops excessive cooling airflow over the engine," according to Lycoming's Ken Johnson. "It is always best to reduce power in increments, so that engine temperature changes will occur gradually."

Of course, on the way down manifold pressure will increase at the same rate as ambient air pressure, which means that in a 500-foot-per-minute descent the throttle *must* be retarded at the rate of one inch of MP every 120 seconds just to keep a constant power setting! (Ambient pressure increases by one inch of mercury for every 1,000-foot drop.)

In airplanes with a significant ram rise, for example turbocharged Cessna twins (Turbo 310, 401, etc.), the mere addition of 20 knots to the indicated airspeed in the initial phase of descent will cause manifold pressure to go up an inch or more, before any altitude (to speak of) has been lost. This brings up the question of whether a descent ought to be initiated with elevator, or throttle. In a "hot" airplane, some throttle reduction is mandatory (to keep from exceeding the sound barrier), but it is unwise to combine a massive throttle reduction with an increase in cooling airflow through the cowling (i.e., increased airspeed). If the airplane has speedbrakes, of course, you should use them. Spoilers, "approach flaps," landing gear (if it can be lowered at fairly high speed), etc., can allow a useful rate of descent at fairly high power without excessive airspeed buildup. Barring that, you simply have to reduce power in small increments—say two inches at a time, with power reductions spaced two minutes apart (or some such).

Some mitigation of the effects of rapid cooling can be had by closing the cowl flaps in the letdown (if present, and if open to begin with). Also, the mixture—if not already at peak EGT—can be adjusted to give peak exhaust temperatures (within limits of TIT). Another good tactic for keeping BMEP reasonably high in the descent (and thus staving off shock cooling) is to reduce rpm in addition to manifold pressure. (This advice is for owners of airplanes with constant-speed propellers.) Reducing rpm increases effective cylinder pressures, all other things being equal. This results in more efficient transfer of heat to the cylinder head, and more even temperatures in the descent.

In a pinch, you can try sideslipping the airplane to lose altitude quickly without chopping power—but use this technique only when you've already tried everything else. Large bending loads are imposed on the prop and crankshaft when sideslipping at airplane at high speed or high BMEPs.

Use common sense when balancing the requirements of the engine against the real-world requirements of Air Traffic Control, collision avoidance, and so forth. *Momentary* power reductions on the order of six or eight inches of manifold pressure (with an appropriate downward adjustment to prop rpm) for purposes of reaching flap-deployment speed, gear-lowering speed, or whatever, need not be harmful to the engine if power is again restored as soon as the flaps and/or landing gear are down. (After all, while you're throttling back, airspeed is decaying quickly and engine cooling is cut commensurately.)

In twins, especially, CHT must be monitored carefully in both climb and descent. Cowl flaps are usually provided for extra cooling airflow through the tiny nacelle. This Cessna Turbo 310's engines (Continental TSIO-520-B) are the same size, weight, and displacement as the TSIO-520 in a Beech B36TC Bonanza, but are crammed into an engine compartment one-third the volume of the Bonanza's. Only smooth operator technique can prevent early top overhauls.

Another trick to remember when it comes to slowing down quickly (for gear lowering) without chopping power or doing a steep "elevator climb" is to *enter* a steep turn while throttling back. This is not something to be tried under instrument conditions. In VFR weather, however, you will probably find occasions on which a deftly timed steep turn can yield important benefits for slowing the airplane. ("Steep" means 45 degrees or so—I'm not suggesting that you do aerobatics.)

Bear in mind that the degree to which power can safely be retarded for descent is probably closely related to the amount of power you were using in cruise to start with. The worst possible case is to go from full rated power (or high cruise power with CHT near the top of the scale) to no power at all; whereas, by contrast, a "sudden reduction" in power from 60 percent to 40 percent is (comparatively speaking) not much of a sudden reduction. Don't be *too* squeamish about bringing the throttle back, especially if you can modulate cooling airflow (airspeed, cowl flaps) in a mitigating fashion. Your job is not to *avoid* CHT changes—since that's clearly impossible—but to husband the thermal inertia of the engine (and other firewall-forward accessories) in a way so as to prevent outright temperature-related or cooling-related damage. That's something that can only be done by timely application of common sense tempered with judgment born of experience.

OVERHEATING

In addition to shock cooling, the operator of a high-performance aircraft engine must be alert to the possibility of cylinder *overheating*, which can come about because of poor operator technique (overleaning, steep climbouts), poor firewall-forward design on the part of the airframe manufacturer (we won't name names), or hot-and-high operating conditions (poor cooling due to high OAT or high density altitude), or mechanical malfunctions of one sort or another.

When the CHT reads frighteningly high, it's impossible hard to know, with a factory CHT (single-probe) system, whether you are experiencing an overtemp condition merely in one jug—the one to which the probe is attached—or in the engine as a whole. With multichannel CHT systems (like that found in the Insight GEM), all mystery is removed. You can tell at a glance how your cylinders are doing, and where, exactly, any problems might lie.

How hot is hot, where CHT is concerned? It's important to understand that with CHT, as with EGT, temperature limits are necessarily somewhat arbitrary, inasmuch as the placement of the probe has a profound effect on the temperature indications seen in the cockpit. Lycoming and Continental do not place their cylinder-head temperature bosses in exactly the same place in their cylinders. Hence, their recommended redlines (or never-exceed CHT recommendations) differ. Lycoming generally prefers 500 degrees Fahrenheit as an upper limit to CHT, while Continental sets the limit at 460 degrees. Lycoming also offers the following advice, in its O-360 Operator's Manual, P/N 60297-12, p. 3-14: "For maximum service life of the engine, maintain cylinder head temperatures between 150 F and 400 F during continuous operation." (In other service literature, Lycoming has stated that continuous operation above 435 degrees on CHT will have a detrimental effect on the TBO life of cylinders.) J.P. Instruments sets the trip-point of its overtemp alarm (on latest versions of the Scanner) at 450 degrees F. This seems reasonable. However, where to set the overtemp threshold is essentially an arbitrary decision.

The point is, the lower the temperature of the cylinder head (within obvious limits), the longer the cylinder head will last, since thermal stresses are less, resulting in less change of shape of metals, less loss of hardness (a problem with aluminum parts subjected to repeated thermal cycles), and so on. There is nothing "magical" about the redline numbers cited above. Your engine will not suddenly come apart if you allow CHT to go to 501 degrees instead of 500. The limitations are set arbitrarily (and somewhat conservatively). I recommend you adhere to them, but don't assume that there is anything *magical* about a particular CHT setpoint.

What should you do when CHT is approaching the upper limits of concern? The immediate answer is to reduce power. Second, enrich mixture. Try a lower cruise alti-

Multiprobe CHT systems, virtually unknown as late as 1984, are slowly coming into demand, as careful operators insist on better, more complete engine instrumentation. The Electronics International gauge shown here is switchable by cylinder (the one shown a few pages earlier is switchable by engine). Multiprobe CHT is primarily useful as a troubleshooting adjunct to multichannel EGT. It often means the difference between seeing a problem develop while it's minor, and finding a dead jug after-the-fact.

tude, if practicable; open cowl flaps; and if possible trim the airplane for a higher airspeed (i.e., apply forward stick; descend).

Reducing power in level flight means reducing airspeed, which would seem at first glance to be a poor thing to do since it cuts cooling airflow. In fact, though, an aircraft engine is much better at producing heat than producing airspeed. It takes a huge increase in power (you've probably noticed) to create even a small increase in airspeed. By throttling back, heat production is cut dramatically with relatively little loss in cooling airflow (especially if cowl flaps can be opened at the same time). So in an overtemp emergency, *always* reduce throttle first.

Descending to a lower altitude may not sound like a good way to counteract CHT, since air is much cooler at altitude; but again, air *density* increases much quicker with each drop in elevation than air *temperature*, and density flow is the parameter of ultimate concern where engine cooling is involved. You can see this effect on your airspeed indicator. At high cruise altitudes, IAS falls dramatically. *So does engine cooling.* Despite higher OATs at low altitude, the denser air makes for more efficient cooling overall. So head down when CHT heads up.

Fuel cooling gives significant cooling to an air-cooled engine; thus, mixture enrichment is desirable during CHT-overtemp emergencies. The effect of mixture adjustments is not as great as the effect of adjustments to throttle, cowl flaps, and airspeed, however. Try the other tricks first, before enrichening the mixture.

When CHT can't be brought under control (for one or all cylinders) by some combination of the foregoing techniques, you may be looking at one or more of the following:

1. Deteriorated cooling baffles (or bird's nests in the intake).

2. An induction air leak.

3. Advanced magneto timing.

4. Fuel pump or carburetor or injector system not set up to give proper fuel flow.

5. Clogged injector nozzles (fuel injected engines only).

6. Detonation (mild or severe).

7. Preignition.

Aggressive leaning of a high-output engine at high power settings is a common cause of too-hot CHTs. In turbocharged engines especially, overly aggressive leaning will lead to detonation. Trace detonation may—in the case of the Navajo's TIO-540-J2BD engine, as well as others—may be encountered even in low-power cruise, at mixtures quite a bit richer than peak. Turbo operators will want to be alert to this.

Bad gasoline (alcohol-diluted autogas, for example) can also cause cylinder overheating, as can carburetor float maladjustment. When the float in a float carburetor rides too high, not enough fuel is metered to the engine for a given airflow (i.e., the carburetor "acts lean") and CHT is often higher than it ought to be.

Occasionally, valves will stop rotating in service. (A mechanism is provided in aircraft engines to spin the valves at a slow, but steady, rate in normal operation, to even up wear at the seat and keep valve faces clean.) Rotation is stopped, typically, by the accumulation of deposits on the back side of the head, which keep the valve from turning in the guide. Regardless of cause, once a valve stops rotating, it eventually will start to burn as carbon deposits (normally brushed away by the rotation of the valve) stick and keep the valve from sealing tightly. Escape of hot exhaust past the burnt valve lip causes the nearby port (whether intake or exhaust) to operate hotter than it normally would. EGT may actually go down, but CHT can shoot up. Obviously, if valve burning is suspected, the plane should be landed as soon as practicable an a thorough investigation made.

TROUBLESHOOTING WITH CHT

Because of the long time lag involved in CHT changes, and because most aircraft do not have multicylinder CHT instrumentation, the troubleshooting possibilities with CHT are somewhat limited. The fast response of EGT is what makes EGT such a valuable troubleshooting aid compared to CHT.

Technically, there is a way around the CHT time lag problem, but it requires a sophisticated software solution, and to date no manufacturer (including Insight) has chosen to implement it. The rate of change of probe temperature is related in a fairly direct way to the amount of heat being applied at the probe: Apply a lot of heat, and the probe undergoes a much faster initial rate of change of temperature than it would if a smaller amount of heat were applied. It is possible to determine (accurately and quickly) the rate of change of CHT probe temperature, and correlate that information with equilibrium probe temperature; it's called looking at the first derivative of the temperature curve. Unfortunately, no one has exploited this tactic for developing a fast-reaction CHT system (which might be useful for spotting detonation, spark plug failure, and a host of other conditions). Any manufacturers out there want to tackle this?

As a troubleshooting tool, CHT is best used in conjunction with EGT, to provide a

For optimum usefulness in troubleshooting, CHT information should be correlated with EGT information. A unit such as the KSA EGT/CHT display shown here can do the job. (Note the overtemp alarm light in the upper left corner of the bezel, and the alarm test button at lower right.) Obviously, all-cylinder display capability would be ideal, but a switchable multiprobe setup is still much better than a single-probe setup.

better-rounded total picture of combustion dynamics. The principal things to bear in mind are the following:

1. If you have only one CHT probe, it's impossible to know what the CHTs of your unprobed cylinders are. Use caution in extrapolating single-probe data to a multicylinder situation.

2. There are many occasions on which CHT will rise even as EGT falls, and vice versa. When a cylinder is detonating, for example, EGT typically falls or stays the same while CHT rises. (This is because of the increased length of time between the end of combustion and the opening of the exhaust valve.) Conversely, CHT will fall—and EGT will rise—when combustion is shifted late, as for example when one spark plug fouls or the magneto timing retards (due to cam follower wear or other problems). Do not assume that because CHT is normal, EGT must be normal; or that because EGT is high, CHT must be high. Consider the total picture.

3. As with EGT, trend information is more important than snapshot information when it comes to CHT. That is to say, the *rate* at which CHT changes is often more important than the *actual value* of the cylinder head temperature at a given moment. Shock cooling, for example, is a *rate* phenomenon, not a *state* phenomenon. The same goes for "shock heating."

4. Cylinder head temperature varies at different points around the cylinder, just as EGT varies at different points in the exhaust pipe. Don't assume that just because the temperature is "within limits" at the probe that your cylinder(s) can't be undergoing abnormal combustion or suffering abnormal thermal or mechanical stresses at the base.

5. CHT should be calibrated periodically. One way to do this is with eutectic solder that melts at a specific temperature. A tab of solder and the CHT probe can be mounted to a heat sink, and the heat sink torched or bathed in hot oil as necessary to achieve the melting temperature of the solder. (Solders of this type can be purchased through scientific supply outlets, such as Omega Engineering. Check your Yellow Pages.) The CHT can then be read and a correlation made. Another, less accurate method involves temperature-sensitive chalk. Go to any welding supply shop or scientific supply store and you'll be able to buy a set of temperature-sensitive marking crayons or chalks, with which you can mark the area adjacent the CHT probe (using several heat ranges of chalk). Operate the engine on the ground just

long enough to make the first chalk turn color; then look at the cockpit CHT gauge.

On the first flight after an overhaul, cylinders should be monitored for barrel temperatures (at the midpoint and at the base, near the hold-down nuts). This is where temperature-sensitive chalks can be quite handy. If chrome rings have been mistakenly installed in chrome barrels, or if oversize pistons have been installed by mistake (creating too little barrel/skirt clearance), or the cylinder is overheating for any other reason, such as detonation or preignition, the change in color of 600-degree chalk will be a tipoff to trouble. This sort of trouble may or may not be corroborated by the head-mounted CHT probe.

Chapter 5
ABNORMAL COMBUSTION

Abnormal combustion can be extremely destructive to an engine, particularly an air-cooled aircraft engine running at or near full power. What's more, it is easily possible, by misuse of the mixture control—as well as through improper maintenance practices—for

Photo shows a typical overleaning-induced failure (in this case, severe erosion of an exhaust valve in a TIO-540, leading to rim failure and loss of a piece of valve through the turbocharger). Notice the severe erosion of metal around the exhaust valve seat and in the combustion chamber dome in general, indicative of sustained detonation.

pilots or mechanics to cause abnormal combustion processes to occur in an aircraft engine. For optimum safe use of an EGT system (and for engine-troubleshooting purposes, too), it is imperative that the pilot know how to detect and avoid abnormal combustion.

In an aircraft engine, abnormal combustion generally falls into one of two categories: detonation or preignition. Much has been said and written about detonation and preignition in aviation circles, and a good deal of misinformation has been propagated. To many pilots, the terms detonation and preignition connote the same thing. In reality, the processes involved are quite distinct; the two phenomena are not the same, although one can bring on the other.

The first systematic studies of detonation and preignition in aircraft engines were conducted by Professor A. H. Gibson in 1915 at the Royal Aircraft Factory at Farnborough, England. Prior to this time, detonation (almost certainly a widespread phenomenon) simply went by the name "overheating." All that was known was that certain engines overheated badly when operating at high specific output using some, but not other, batches of gasoline.

The term "knock" was not known to pilots, since a detonating aircraft engine could not be heard to ping or clatter over the already deafening sound of propellers, valving, gearing, and unmuffled exhaust. To detect detonation, cylinder head temperature was monitored—most often visually. Standard practice in Gibson's own lab was to monitor detonation by observing the extent to which cylinder heads glowed red during night test-stand runs. Professor Gibson noted that overheating (detonation) was seemingly lessened by enrichening the fuel/air mixture. He also noted that benzol-blended fuels—and aromatic fuels in general—were less likely to cause overheating than straight-run gasolines.

In 1919, Harry Ricardo was contracted by the Asiatic Petroleum Company (a member of the Shell group) to conduct research into detonation and its relation to fuel characteristics. Ricardo, assisted by consulting physicists David Pye and Henry T. Tizard, designed a variable-compression test engine and set about investigating the relationship of engine performance to physical and chemical properties of various fuels. Among the conclusions immediately reached by Ricardo's group were that, first, the chemical composition of a fuel could indeed exert a profound influence on the performance of the engine, as expected; secondly, the actual differences between fuels in terms of power output *without* detonation was rather small, only about 4 percent; and thirdly, the more detonation-resistant the fuel, the higher the compression ratio that could be employed (thus the greater the maximum engine output).

Ricardo's explanation of detonation, given in his 1923 text *The Internal Combustion Engine*, is just as valid today as it was in the early Twenties: "When the rate of temperature rise due to compression by the burning portion of the charge exceeds that at which it can get rid of its heat by conduction, convection, etc. by a certain margin, the remaining portion ignites spontaneously throughout its whole bulk, thus setting up an explosion wave which strikes the walls of the cylinder with a hammer-like blow and reacting in its turn, compresses afresh the portion first ignited. This further raises the temperature of that portion and with it the temperature of any isolated or partially isolated objects in its vicinity, thus ultimately giving rise to preignition." Even in 1923, preignition was known to be a separate phenomenon—with its own mode of action—distinct from detonation. Preignition, as the name implies, is nothing more than the premature lightoff of a fuel-air charge by a hot ignition source in the combustion chamber, usually not the spark plug. Detonation is a much more subtle concept.

While Gibson, Ricardo, *et al* were performing pioneering research in the U.K., the Dayton Engineering Laboratories (Delco) in the U.S. had begun focusing research dollars on a serious and seemingly incurable overheating problem in General Motors lighting generator sets running on kerosene. Delco researchers noted with consternation and surprise that the supposedly superior-quality Pennsylvanian kerosenes consistently caused detonation, whereas the relatively cheap illuminating-grade kerosenes made from Californian crude stocks did not cause overheating. The Delco-Lites (as they were known) operated off a newly designed battery ignition system that GM's Charles Kettering had created for automotive use, to replace troublesome magnetos. Delco's initial inclination was to blame the Delco-Lite generator overheating on the new Kettering ignition. Kettering, however, wisely suspected the fuel as the source of the trouble. He and his assistant, Thomas Midgely, began investigating the detonation properties of a wide variety of fuels, using a standard (air-cooled) Delco-Lite engine modified to take different cylinder heads for varying the compression ratio. Kettering and Midgely verified the effect of compression ratio on knock (namely, an increase in compression ratio brings with it an increase in the likelihood of knock; conversely, a

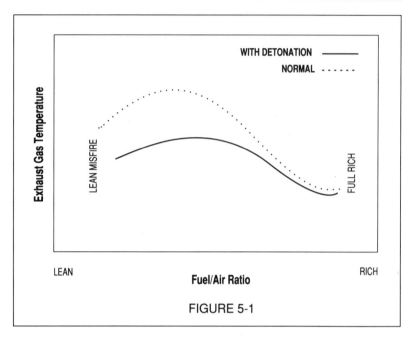

WITH DETONATION ——————
NORMAL · · · · · ·

FIGURE 5-1

Detonation (combustion knock) causes a flattening of the EGT curve, which is seen in the cockpit as a "peak that never peaks." The peak temperature is lower because more of the exhaust gas's heat has been transferred to the cylinder head than normal, and because the combustion end-gases have had a longer period of time to cool.

decrease in compression ratio allows the knock-free use of a wider variety of fuels)—but they also discovered that the molecular architecture of the fuel molecules played a critical role in the knocking tendency of the fuel.

The family of compounds known as hydrocarbons includes many different individual molecular species, all with the common property that carbon atoms link together to form the backbone of the molecule, with hydrogen atoms attached like Christmas ornaments to the carbon atoms. (No hydrogen-hydrogen bonding occurs. Only carbon-hydrogen and carbon-carbon bonding are allowed.) In molecules with more than four carbon atoms, the carbons may be arranged either linearly, or in a branched (forked) fashion. At higher molecular weights, the carbons may even link in such a way as to form a cyclic or looped compound. Work by Kettering and Midgely, and also Graham Edgar of Ethyl Gasoline Corporation, determined that the knock tendency of a given pure hydrocarbon fuel depended not just on molecular weight (overall length of the carbon chain), but the *shape* (straight, branched, cyclic) of the molecule's carbon-carbon "backbone." The worst offenders for knocking, it was found, were linear-type hydrocarbons (also called "normal" hydrocarbons or 'n-' isomers). The hydrocarbons *least* likely to knock, researchers learned, were those with significant branching of the carbon-carbon backbone (including "iso-" compounds, such as iso-octane).

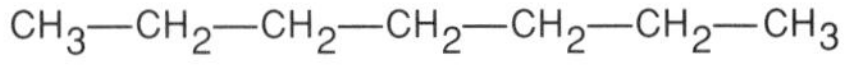

Graham Edgar applied this knowledge in a systematic study of pure hydrocarbons that re-

$$CH_3—CH_2—CH_2—CH_2—CH_2—CH_2—CH_3$$

n-heptane (octane rating: 0)

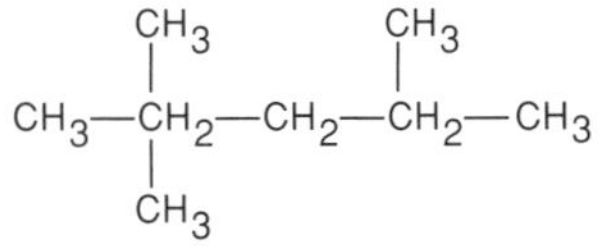

$$CH_3—\underset{\underset{CH_3}{|}}{\overset{\overset{CH_3}{|}}{CH_2}}—CH_2—\underset{}{\overset{\overset{CH_3}{|}}{CH_2}}—CH_3$$

iso-octane (octane rating: 100)

FIGURE 5-2

Graham Edgar's octane rating system uses two reference fuels, normal heptane (top) and iso-octane (bottom), one representing zero octane and the other, 100 octane. A test fuel that duplicates the knock performance of an X:Y blend of iso-octane and heptane (where X + Y = 100) is said to have an octane rating of 'X'. (Example: A fuel that duplicates the knock performance of an iso-octane/heptane blend consisting of 87% iso-octane and 13% heptane would be said to have an octane rating of 87.)

sulted in his proposal, in 1927, of a knock-performance standard based on two specific reference fuels. Edgar had found that a straight-chain seven-carbon compound called normal heptane (n-heptane) would cause detonation under almost all conditions even in a knock-resistant engine; he proposed that n-heptane be awarded a score of zero on a 0-100 rating scale. The best, most knock-resistant fuel Edgar had come up with was a branched eight-carbon compound called iso-octane; he proposed that *this* fuel be given a score of 100. Since these two reference fuels had almost identical characteristics where volatility and physical properties were concerned, it was a simple matter to blend them in any proportion necessary to arrive at a mix that would exactly match the knocking tendency of any sample fuel or "test" fuel that needed to be rated. Edgar proposed that the percentage (by volume) of iso-octane in a blend of iso-octane and n-heptane that gave a blend that duplicated a given fuel's performance in a test engine should consistute that fuel's "score" from zero to 100 on an "octane scale." For example, under this system, if a particular fuel such as ethyl alcohol were found to knock to the same extent as a 90:10 mixture of iso-octane and heptane, then ethyl alcohol would be said to have an "octane rating" of 90. This is the famous octane scale with which every automobile owner in the world is familiar.

It should be noted that determining the octane score of a fuel *always* requires that the fuel be run in a test engine. "Octane" is an empirical concept. There is no easy way to predict a fuel's knock performance, other than to actually run it in an engine to see if it knocks, and how much. (For this reason, there will never be an easy field test for airplane owners to determine the antiknock suitability of autogas for a given airplane. Octane *must* be determined empirically—the fuel must be burned in an engine, and its knock limits found that way.)

TETRAETHYL LEAD

The early research by Kettering and Midgely led to another outstanding result which ought not to go undiscussed. Kettering and Midgely, in the course of their Delco-Lite experiments, had noted that the addition of a small amount of iodine to "bad" kerosene had a profound anti-knock effect on the fuel. Not long after this discovery was made, General Motors assigned Midgely to undertake a research program to isolate compounds that might be added to hydrocarbon fuels to suppress detonation. In one of the most impressive chemical-screening efforts of the era, Midgely (aided by his assistant, Thomas A. Boyd) screened more than 30,000 chemicals of all types before eventually hitting on tetraethyl lead as a potent knock-inhibitor during an engine test on December 9, 1921. (Midgely had decided to concentrate on organometallic compounds, of which TEL is one, for the simple reason that a seemingly likely theory for explaining detonation had it that radiation from the flame overheated the combustion chamber walls to cause preignition. Organometallic dyes were thought to introduce opacity to the combustion gases, and cut down flame radiation. This theory has since fallen into disrepute.)

The discovery of the remarkable antiknock properties of tetraethyl lead (TEL) will surely rank as one of the most momentous discoveries of the technological era. The use of "lead" (actually TEL) in fuels was a driving factor in the development of the modern high-compression spark-ignition engine. (Early Allied use of highly leaded aviation fuels shaped the outcome of the Battle of Britain, and indeed of World War

II itself.) Without tetraethyl lead, the economical development of efficient, high-compression piston engines—for cars, trucks, planes, boats, chain saws, motorcycles, ground-power units, etc.—would have been delayed or even made impossible. Extensive research by oil companies after Midgely's initial discovery of TEL failed miserably to yield a better, more potent antiknock additive.

Even today, TEL's exact mode of action in suppressing the chemical processes responsible for detonation are not well understood. (If they were, chemists would be able to model even better, more efficient molecules and the search for a truly cheap, safe, environmentally sound knock suppressor could begin in earnest.) It *is* clear that the lead atom, not the ethyl radicals, is responsible for TEL's antiknock effect, since other gasoline-soluble lead compounds give antiknock action (though none as efficiently as TEL). Most lead compounds, of course, are not even soluble in gasoline.

RICH VERSUS LEAN OCTANE RATINGS

We mentioned earlier that rating a fuel's octane (antiknock) quality involves running it in an engine; the knock rating of a fuel is something that can only be arrived at empirically. We also mentioned that mixture (F/A ratio) has a definite effect on knock suppression—one of the early outcomes of Gibson's 1915 detonation research.

The question arises, what fuel/air mixture should be used in the standard test procedure to rate a fuel by the octane method? If the "test engine" is rich-running, after all, or if it is operating at very low rpms and manifold pressures, a falsely low indication will be given of the test-fuel's knocking tendency. Exactly this problem was encountered soon after the introduction of Graham Edgar's famous octane scale. In England in 1937, during the development of the 12-cylinder Rolls-Royce Merlin engine (a highly supercharged aircraft engine), high-test aviation gasoline had to be imported from the United States, since there were no refineries in Great Britain capable of making 100-octane gas. Rolls-Royce, aware of the potential for knock, provided considerable mixture enrichment for the new Merlin. But soon after Rolls began testing the Merlin on U.S.-made gas, wide variations were found in what was called the "rich mixture response" of the fuel. From a detonation standpoint, the fuel was of poorer quality than expected.

The unanticipated poor performance of U.S. gas posed a serious impediment to the development of the Merlin engine (as well as the Bristol Pegasus and Hercules engines). Although detonation could be controlled by enrichening the mixture, the British—having already provided significant mixture enrichment—were hesitant to enrichen any further, especially when it was obvious that what was needed was better control over fuel quality. American oil companies had been rating gasolines for octane in test engines running at very low manifold pressures compared to the new British military aircraft engines, and it was obvious that a change in test procedures would be needed; existing antiknock tests were not rigorous enough.

A decision was made to add a new category of octane test to the existing one. The new "rich-mixture" procedure, or supercharge method, was adopted in 1942 and resulted in the creation of so-called Performance Numbers for gasoline. Performance Numbers were invented to allow octane numbers higher than 100. (Obviously, in the octane rating method as originally proposed by Graham Edgar, no fuel can have a score higher than 100 since the 100-octane reference is iso-octane. Edgar had no way of knowing that hydrocarbons and additive packages would someday be created which would result in some fuels having better antiknock performance than pure iso-octane.) In the supercharge test, the antiknock performance of the test fuel is compared to that of an iso-octane/TEL blend. A fuel that might have scored 100 on the standard (Edgar) octane scale, using the so-called "lean method" test conditions (low manifold pressure, etc.) might well have a rich-mixture, supercharge-method Performance Number of 130; hence 100/130 avgas.

The lean-mixture and rich-mixture (or supercharge method) octane tests have been retained to this day, with minor variations over the years. Somewhat different test engines and testing conditions are used in rating automotive gasolines; the methods now in use are the Motor and Research methods. The octane number displayed on American gas pumps is generally the arithmetic-average of Motor and Research octane ratings (M+R/2). This corresponds approximately to the lean-mixture octane rating used in aviation.

OCTANE ANOMALIES

Some idea of the subtlety of the octane concept can be gained from consideration of the fact that three different fuels, each with the same lean-method octane rating, can easily give three widely different results in the supercharge or rich-mixture test. (For example, it is possible for one fuel to score 87 on the rich-mixture octane test and another to score 92, even though both score 80 by the lean method.) The amount of "spread" between octane ratings by different methods is referred to, in the oil industry, as a fuel's "sensitivity." Highly aromatic fuels such as unleaded American autogas exhibit high sensitivity. Paraffinic fuels (straight-run gasolines) are less sensitive.

Different fuel stocks exhibit different sensitivities to TEL's antiknock effect, as well. The additional of one milliliter of TEL to a gallon of straight-run gasoline will have a greater octane-boosting effect than the addition of one ml of TEL to a gallon of alcohol-blended gasoline.

Generally speaking, however, regardless of the starting fuel, each successive dose of TEL adds a smaller increment of antiknock performance; the first small additions of TEL have the most antiknock effect. TEL's dose-response curve is not linear.

Another interesting outcome of octane research is that engine performance, in terms of knock-limiting horsepower (or knock-limiting max BMEP, or max allowable manifold pressure) is not a linear function of increasing octane. That is to say, as knock-limiting horsepower is plotted against fuel octane number, an upward-bending curve is obtained (not a straight line), up to 100 octane. Above 100 octane, the rate of power enhancement falls off faster than straightline fashion with increasing TEL. What this means (if you're an engine designer) is that by designing an engine to use 100-octane fuel instead of 80-octane, you can expect more than just a 20 or 25-percent specific-power increase. (The increase is more like 30 percent; it is not a simple 100:80 ratio.) But at the lower octanes, say 50 or 60, a 20-point increase in the fuel's antiknock rating gives only about a 10-percent increase in knock-limiting compression ratio. The performance benefits of increasing octane start out small, at the low-octane end of the scale, and become much bigger as higher numbers are reached. To put it yet another way: A one-point octane gain in a high-octane fuel yields much bigger performance gains (in real terms *and* in percentage terms) than a one-point gain in a low-octane fuel. The higher octane numbers are "bigger."

It is important to understand, however, that extra power does not arise from the mere use of higher-octane gasoline in an engine not designed for it. Higher octane merely makes possible the use of higher-compression cylinders or pistons, more turbo boost, etc., without engine knock. Putting 100-octane gas into an engine designed for 80-octane will not give the engine any extra power at all. Nor will it cause the engine to run hotter. *Octane* refers only to the antiknock qualities of the fuel.

One more thing to consider: Two fuels that give identical performance in a test engine (by the Motor Method, or whatever) very often do not give comparable performance in a real engine operating in the real world. Conversely, two different engines may show marked differences in knock onset using the same fuel, even though compression ratios, timing advance, and BMEP, etc. may be the same for each engine. Such things as combustion chamber shape, valve positioning, the number and position of spark plugs, and other even more subtle factors play an important role in determining the antiknock performance of various fuels in various engines in the real world. (As an example of this, angle-valve cylinder heads are more detonation-resistant than parallel-valve heads; and rounded or hemispherical combustion chambers are more knock-resistant than squarish, flat-headed designs. Also, the use of dual spark plugs makes possible higher knock-limiting compression ratios.)

With careful attention to cylinder design, it is possible to achieve knock-free combustion on unleaded gasolines at compression ratios as high as 11.5:1.

DETONATION'S MODE OF ACTION

What, you may ask, do we know about the mechanism or mode of action of detonation? How does it come about? We know that it involves spontaneous combustion of a portion of the fuel-air mixture (or charge) in the cylinder, at some point distant from the spark plug; and we know it results in a very rapid, sharp pressure rise in the cylinder (which gives the familiar metallic knock or ping). Ricardo likened the abnormal combustion process to an explosion. This may not seem a very edifying analogy if one's concept of internal combustion is that fuel and air *naturally* explode upon ignition. In reality, fuel and air *do not* explode during normal combustion. Instead, there is slow, even, continuous burning of the fuel; the flame spreads outward (at a fairly slow rate; six to 20 feet per second) from the spark plug and arrives at distant points of the combustion chamber fractions of a second after ignition. This is not the same as an explosion. An explosion is where the *entire* fuel-air charge ignites all at once, everywhere in the combustion chamber.

The actual flame-front velocity of a burning gasoline-air mixture varies over a fairly wide range of values (as you'd expect) depending on *temperature and pressure.* If you put a match to a pool of gasoline at sea level, in the open air, you will find that the flame front travels quite slowly—about three feet per second. If, on the other hand, you compress the fuel and air vapors together before igniting them, you find that the flame front travels much faster away from the ignition source.

It is worth pondering the situation as it occurs in an engine, where flame-front speeds of 10 to 20 feet per second are common, again depending on pre-spark (and post-spark!) pressures and temperatures. It is a happy accident of fate that as pre-spark charge pressures are reduced by throttling back to lower manifold pressures, flame speeds slow as well, thereby preventing peak combustion pressures from drifting early. Were combustion to "peak out" as quickly at idle rpm as it does at full throttle, your engine might kick back and run backwards. (Your spark plugs, after all, fire well before the piston reaches top center; ignition occurs at about 25 degrees BTC.) As it turns out, flame speed increases fortuitously with engine rpm, so that peak combustion pressure occurs always at about 16 degrees of crank travel after top center (ATC) in the power stroke. Under normal conditions.

Detonation, which is explosionlike in its suddenness, is not a normal condition, obviously. It occurs *after* normal spark ignition, and yet it also causes combustion to be finished well before the normal p_{max} angle of 16 degrees. (Any burning or exploding that occurs *before* spark-plug discharge is, of course, preignition, by definition.) We might ask what is the "secondary ignition source" that causes detonation to occur after normal spark plug initiation of combustion.

Usually secondary ignition is pressure-related, although hot spots in the combustion chamber can also hasten a secondary lightoff. The temperature and pressure rise caused by post-ignition charge compression—compression of the *unburned* fuel-air charge by the *combusted* portion of charge—is usually what sets off the explosion.

This really requires nothing more than elementary physics to explain. Expanding exhaust gases (mostly carbon dioxide and steam) exert a pressure on the unburned charge, compressing it and heating it. If the fuel is of poor quality (i.e., high in straight-chain hydrocarbons), it undergoes a type of thermal cracking—breakage into fragments (radicals)—and autoignites. The shock wave from the autoignition of the charge then sends vibrations throughout the cylinder and piston (and engine), and you have "knock." If the fuel is of good quality and high in branched-structure hydrocarbons, spontaneous thermal cracking doesn't occur, and you don't get any knocking.

Perhaps the most important thing to understand is that detonation brings with it abnormally high instantaneous cylinder pressures and temperatures. These pressures and temperatures can lead to localized overheating of exhaust valves, valve deposits, spark plug tips, lead deposits inside the combustion chamber, small folds of metal leftover from machining new cylinder parts, etc., creating tiny red-hot areas that may promote and intensify the knocking process, or even (in severe cases) instantly ignite incoming fuel and air on the next intake event. When the incoming charge ignites prematurely (that is, before the spark plug has had a chance to fire), and *only* then, the engine is said to be experiencing *preignition*.

Preignition and detonation are—as you can well appreciate—potentially very destructive, but the effects they produce can vary. Whereas preignition is an all-or-nothing affair (you're either having it or you're not), detonation can be serious or light or moderate in intensity and can last a short time or a long time, depending on operating conditions. Severe detonation, left uncorrected, will result in catastrophic failure of piston rings, pistons, or other top-end parts in a matter of minutes. Light to moderate detonation, if corrected in time, will not necessarily fail an engine, but the effects will be cumulative over time. That is, an engine that has experienced numerous episodes of light to moderate detonation will accumulate stresses (and dimensional changes) in valves, pistons, piston rings, connecting rods, con rod bolts, etc., which may lead to early component retirement or outright failure.

Preignition in an aircraft engine usually leads to catastrophic failure of critical engine parts within seconds. This is partly because of abnormal stresses, and partly because of abnormal temperatures. Not only are the stresses created during preignition extremely damaging (because of the sheer magnitude of the pressure pulses), but the high temperatures involved are quite apt to create additional secondary hot spots in the combustion chamber which further feed the preignition process, causing more hot spots, more preignition, etc. (hence the term "runaway preignition")—indeed leading, often, to outright meltdown of aluminum pistons. After piston burning or holing, combustion flames are free to enter the crankcase, and it's good-bye, engine. Maybe good-bye, airplane as well.

How can you tell if your engine is experiencing preignition? In all likelihood, you'll know by the loss of power (and/or the flames coming out of the engine compartment). Barring that, your EGT indications will be "topped out"—fullscale max-hot. Also you may be feeling abnormal vibrations and hearing unusual noises from ahead of the firewall. With any of these indications, your first reaction should be to *throttle* back (then enrichen the mixture). Throttling back is the single most important thing you can do.

Detonation is harder to detect than preignition. If it is severe enough, of course, you will feel and hear its effects in terms of power deterioration, vibration, and an increase in noise from ahead of the firewall, the same as in a car. Most times, however, detonation goes unnoticed by the pilot since it is often light in intensity and transient in occurrence, and normal engine and prop noises obscure the "knocking" produced by it. (Also, trace detonation may only on one cylinder only, while the other, richer cylinders behave normally.) Probably the most reliable indicator of detonation is EGT. (CHT will go up eventually, but the thermal inertia of the cylinder head is such that a detonation episode may already be over by the time CHT indications change.) When detonation occurs, exhaust gas temperature as measured at the EGT probe goes down.

Why does indicated EGT go down (instead of up) when detonation is occurring? Because the combustion event is finished well in advance of the normal time. Instead of combustion taking, say, 3 milliseconds and 50 degrees of crankshaft travel to reach the 90% completion point, it now takes one millisecond and 20 degrees of crank travel to reach completion. More time is available for the cylinder head (and valves, pistons, rings, etc.) to absorb the heat produced in combustion/ explosion, and that heat is more efficiently transferred at the higher pressures involved. (The greater transfer of heat to the cylinder head is reflected in the higher CHT.) By the time the exhaust gases reaches the EGT probe, they've cooled significantly. Indicated EGT thus drops.

Suppose you have taken off with one fuel tank filled with 100LL avgas, and another fuel tank filled with autogas of questionable octane value. On reaching cruise altitude, you lean the engine to peak EGT, then switch tanks from avgas to autogas. (We assume for purposes of this example that the auto fuel is alcohol-free and has the same latent energy content as the avgas.) How will you know if detonation is occurring on autogas? Watch the EGT. If indicated EGT drops 50 degrees or more when autogas is selected, you have reason to suspect

Turbocharged engines, especially non-intercooled ones like the Navajo Chieftain's Lycoming TIO-540-J2BD, are more prone to detonation than normally aspirated engines of the same displacement, because of the high manifold pressures and elevated compressor discharge temperatures generated by the turbo compressor. (The TIO-540-J2BD operates at cruise manifold pressures as high as 40 inches.) See Figs. 2-2 and 2-3 for detonation characteristics of the Navajo Chieftain's engine.

detonation. If CHT rises shortly thereafter, you have confirmed the diagnosis.

Will all cylinders' EGT drop an equal amount? No. Remember, some of your cylinders are richer than others. Also, some have greater amounts of deposits, hotter or cooler exhaust valves, etc., than others; and these things will affect detonation. (In addition, TEL from the fuel is by no means evenly distributed to all cylinders of a carbureted engine.) It is quite possible, when operating at or very near the point of detonation onset—either with autogas or avgas—for just one cylinder to detonate. Likewise, it is possible to experience *preignition* in only one cylinder. (One is all it takes, as far as serious engine damage goes.) This is yet another reason why it is important to have EGT and CHT probes for *all* cylinders. It enables you to crosscheck cylinder indications, one against the other, and detect potentially disastrous combustion anomalies that might otherwise go unnoticed until it's too late.

What remedial action can you take to lessen or eliminate detonation when it is occurring? The very best course of action is to reduce power (if practicable). The second-most-effective thing you can do is enrichen the mixture. Almost any detonation episode can be halted by a combination of reducing power and enrichening the mixture.

Of course, the best action is prevention. Don't use fuel of questionable octane value, watch line attendants to make sure they are not introducing jet fuel to your tanks, and don't lean your engine excessively at high power settings. (Lycoming also advises operators to avoid using full carburetor heat at high power settings, due to the fact that super-hot intake air encourages detonation.) Good maintenance is important, too. An overly lean carburetor or fuel injection system—or partially plugged injector nozzles—will reduce detonation margins, as will improperly advanced magneto timing.

FACTORS THAT AFFECT DETONATION

We have seen that fuel quality and compression ratio have a definite, pronounced effect on detonation; i.e., the higher the compression ratio of the engine, the more likely the engine is to detonate on a given grade of gasoline (or conversely, the higher the octane rating of the gas, the greater will be the knock-limiting compression ratio of the engine). The mechanism of detonation helps explain the compression-ratio effect. After all, it is the *compression heating* of the unburned charge that promotes detonation. Anything that tends to promote premature heating of the unburned charge—whether by compression or by other methods—will naturally encourage autoignition of the charge (i.e., detonation).

Among other things, this means that overheating of the combustion chamber itself will encourage detonation. Obviously, if valves or engine deposits are overheated (perhaps not to the point of glowing cherry-red and causing outright preignition, but sufficiently overheated to encourage detonation), then autoignition of the unburned charge will be promoted. Likewise, if pre-spark cylinder pressures are high enough, detonation will occur a split-second after spark-plug discharge. This is another way of saying that *high power settings* encourage detonation. A more accurate statement, however, is that *high brake mean effective pressures* tend to promote detonation. Brake mean effective pressure is a measure of the average cylinder pressure of an engine. "Brake" refers to brake horsepower (or power determined by a brake method). Brake mean effective pressure, or BMEP, is *directly* proportional to horsepower output, and inversely proportional to rpm and displacement. In other words, if two engines have the same displacement (say 360 cubic inches) and are producing the same horsepower (say 180-hp), the slower-turning engine is operating at a higher BMEP. In automotive parlance, the slower engine is "lugging." And it is more apt to detonate.

Any pre-heating of the fuel-air charge on its way to the combustion chamber is a definite invitation to detonation. How might such pre-heating occur? Carburetor heat is one possibility; turbocharging is another. The former will produce a temperature rise at the carburetor of 90 degrees Fahrenheit or more; the latter may result in intake-air temperatures as high as 300 degrees. It is impossible to specify any single "manifold temperature" as a safe cutoff point, above which detonation is to be expected, since fuel quality and engine design (and maintenance, and operation) vary so much. Nonetheless, the pilot should at least be aware of the fact that intake air temperatures have a definite effect on detonation margins. High temperatures reduce them.

Advanced magneto timing also lessens detonation margins (increases detonation likelihood), at least in engines that are operating on the retarded side of best-power-timing (which aircraft engines are). Normal wear of magneto breaker points can contribute to advanced timing; and of course, sloppy maintenance can result in a mistimed magneto. The sharp pilot will pick this up as a reduced mag drop on runup. Also, EGTs will be higher with advanced ignition. CHTs will be higher, too—much higher, if detonation gets a chance to start.

The effect of mixture on detonation is more subtle. Certainly, excessive leaning at high power settings will induce detonation (simply because higher combustion-chamber temperatures and pressures are being produced). It is not strictly accurate, however, to say that lean mixtures are—in general—more apt to detonate than rich mixtures. Extensive research by Texaco and others has shown that ultra-high-compression-ratio spark-ignition engines can only run knock-free *with* ultra-lean mixtures. Very lean mixtures burn slowly and are slow, also, to autoignite. This is the key to understanding the so-called *stratified charge* approach to engine design, in which excellent fuel economies are obtained (via high compression ratios) by using a small, rich area of charge as the lightoff zone to ignite an overall very lean mixture. Typically, a small "pilot" injector nozzle (secondary to the main fuel injector nozzle) provides the cylinder with a rich zone near the spark plug(s) for ignition of what is otherwise a very lean charge—too lean, in fact, to ignite with a spark. When the charge is stratified in this manner (with a rich zone near one end of the combustion chamber and a lean zone at the opposite end), compression of the unburned charge does not result in autoignition (detonation). The engine, in fact, operates smoothly at high power, with excellent fuel economy, at overall extremely lean mixtures—with no detonation.

Teledyne Continental is exploiting a variant of the charge-stratification scheme in its liquid-cooled (IOL- and TIOL-series) engines, which operate knock-free at 11-to-1 compression ratio thanks not only to liquid cooling of the cylinder but to the use of "swirl chambers" in the cylinder head. Fuel and air, once injected, swirl at great speed in special pockets in the heads, in effect centrifuging the mixture. The spark plugs are located at the periphery of the swirl chamber, where the charge is richest. After lightoff, the remaining ultra-lean portion of charge burns without detonating.

In summary, factors that affect the detonation tendencies of an engine include (among others) the following:

1. Fuel composition.
2. Compression ratio of the engine.
3. Brake mean effective pressure (or power setting).
4. Ignition timing.
5. Intake-air temperature.
6. Combustion chamber temperature (cylinder cooling, CHT).
7. Cylinder compression (or lack of it).
8. Mixture setting (at high BMEPs).
9. Number of operating spark plugs.
10. Combustion chamber design (angle-valve vs. parallel), mixture stratification.
11. Deposit buildups.

Remember that detonation makes EGT go down, while preignition makes EGT shoot up (offscale max-hot). Detonation can lead to preignition, but they are not the same phenomenon. When encountering either one in flight, reduce power immediately; check mixture second.

Chapter 6

TROUBLESHOOTING WITH EGT

The multicylinder EGT/CHT system is one of the most powerful engine-troubleshooting tools available to pilots—or mechanics. (If the multiprobe EGT hadn't been invented for cockpit use, it probably would have been developed for repair diagnostics and sold to maintenance shops on that basis.) The system is only as "smart," however, as the pilot who is using it. Considerable skill in interpretation is sometimes called for in the diagnosis of engine problems by the EGT method. It is not something that can be learned by rote, or done by looking at a chart in a cookbook. The purpose of this chapter is not to impart simple cause-and-effect mnemonics or develop kneejerk responses to potentially complex problems. To get the most out of your multiprobe EGT requires not only that you understand the nature of the combustion process in the context of normal reciprocating aircraft engine operation (which we've already spent a good deal of this book talking about), but also the manner in which the EGT system itself gathers and displays information. Unless you understand how an instrument senses what it senses and displays what it displays, you can't hope to intelligently interpret that instrument's indications even under *normal* circumstances, let alone during periods of troubleshooting.

WHAT DOES AN EGT PROBE MEASURE?

Before we delve into advanced EGT analysis and troubleshooting, let us consider the deceptively simple question of just what it is that an EGT thermocouple senses. Certainly, it responds to temperature changes (heat) in the exhaust pipe. Thermocouples have the interesting property (as explained in Chapter 1) of producing a small voltage which varies with temperature; the higher the temperature of the dissimilar-metal junction, the greater the voltage across that junction. Each particular metal alloy has its own particular electronegativity, or tendency to accept or donate electrons relative to other alloys, and in theory at least, any two dissimilar metals—when joined together—give a thermocouple.

The probe itself is bathed by hot exhaust gases when the exhaust valve opens. But you'll recall that in a four-stroke-cycle (Otto cycle) engine, the exhaust valve spends approximately two-thirds of its operating time in the closed position. Hence, the EGT probe spends two-thirds of its time sensing—what? Residual exhaust heat? Radiant heat from the cylinder head? Nothing at all? One can picture the EGT probe sitting idle approximately two-thirds of the time, then being blasted with a scorching-hot, high-pressure "pulse" of exhaust gas (containing carbon dioxide, water vapor, nitrogen, oxides of nitrogen, soot, ozone, carbon monoxide, acids, aldehydes, ketones, and a zoo of other minority combustion products), at the time of exhaust-valve opening. The exhaust gas, of course, is in the process of expanding when it leaves the combustion chamber. Hence it is cooling even as it passes the probe.

Already we can see that when we speak of "temperature at the EGT probe," we're speaking of some kind of *average* temperature. Obviously the gas surrounding the probe is hottest when it is just emerging from the combustion chamber; in the interval between exhaust-valve closing and valve opening, the effective temperature is much lower, because the gas is expanding, radiating heat, and passing heat by convection into surrounding pipes (and probes). Also, there is wind chill to consider. The high speed of the outrushing exhaust gases (at the moment of valve opening) causes the probe surface to heat up very fast—much faster than it cools down *between* power cycles—for the same reason that an icy wind in the wintertime makes you feel as if it's much colder than it really is. How fast the probe heats up depends not only on probe mass (the more massive it is, the slower its response time), but also its surface area. All things being equal, the probe with the greatest ratio of surface area to mass will give the fastest response time—and also the highest indicated EGT. Conversely, the engine or cylinder with the greatest exhaust *outflow velocity* will have the highest apparent EGT. (You might ask yourself what the effect would be on EGT if your engine were fitted with larger, or smaller, valves.)

If you are confused by all these factors, don't be. The key thing to note is that the EGT probe is *exposed to a regularly recurring cycle of events.* The probe is alternately being blasted with hot, high-speed gases, then allowed to cool. (The only reason your EGT doesn't flicker in the cockpit is that the combustion cycle is of overall shorter duration than the response time of the probe.) You're seeing a rough moving average of the temperature of a small amount of metal (i.e., the thermocouple junction) sitting in the exhaust pipe. You are *not* seeing the "actual" temperature of the exhaust gases—you're merely seeing the average temperature of the *probe* over many combustion/exhaust cycles. (The probe doesn't "know" the temperature of the exhaust; it only "knows" its own temperature.) The reason the information given to us by the probe is useful is that it reflects a recurring, predictable cycle of events, a cycle that—when disrupted by mechanical malfunction or abnormal combustion—gives predictable changes in EGT.

TIMING EFFECTS

Consider the normal combustion cycle. The intake valve opens just as the exhaust valve is about to shut, with the piston moving upward on the exhaust stroke; on the piston's next downstroke, fuel and air are drawn into the cylinder. On the ensuing compression upstroke, naturally, both valves are closed. About 25 degrees of crankshaft rotation before the piston reaches top center, the spark plugs discharge. Two flame fronts (one per ignition source) spread outward from the plug electrodes. The continuing upward movement of the piston, and the expansion of the burned portion of fuel-air charge, exert pressure on the piston—and on the unburned charge. Peak combustion pressure occurs just after the piston passes top center—perhaps 15 or 20 crank degrees after top center (the exact amount will vary, depending on engine rpm and other factors). At this critical moment—the moment of peak combustion pressure—the pressure inside the cylinder may well be 600 psi or more (a total force of several tons, on a 5-inch-diameter piston), and combustion temperatures are of the order 4,000 degrees Fahrenheit, easily enough to melt aluminum. Your pistons do not melt, however, because they are exposed to the 4,000-degree peak temperature only at the surface, and only for a few thousandths of a second. Oil cooling, air and fuel cooling by incoming (unburned) charge, the slowness of the piston to absorb heat, etc., causes the piston to reach equilibrium at something far less than its melting temperature (fortunately).

Around 50 degrees or so of crank travel before the piston reaches bottom on the power stroke, the exhaust valve opens. Only now does the EGT probe—sitting a few inches outside the combustion chamber—get a "peek" at the remnants of combustion. By this point, of course, the combustion gases that a few milliseconds ago (about 120 crankshaft degrees ago) were 4,000 or more degrees have expanded and cooled to a considerable extent, and as the exhaust valve opens they expand further (and cool further). In addition, heat is being thrown off from the gases to the surrouding engine components. So by the time the gases reach the EGT probe, they're perhaps 1,800 degrees. Wind chill is considerable, but the probe can only absorb heat so fast, and anyway spends much of its time cooling down between combustion cycles—so the probe reaches (let's say) 1,400 degrees in this example.

When it comes to troubleshooting an engine problem, nothing beats having an all-cylinder EGT/CHT display. The KSA unit shown here flipflops between CHT mode and EGT mode for quick comparison of data by cylinder. Dials at the bottom are for "zeroing" the needles, which can be useful when an intermittent problem is suspected.

The key thing to notice is that if engine rpm, mixture, manifold pressure, and all other operating parameters are left the same, an equilibrium will be reached such that the EGT probe (and CHT probe, and in fact all engine parts) will remain at a steady temperature.

Conversely, *if any operating parameter is changed, the equilibrium temperature(s) will change.*

Given the sequence of events just described, it should be obvious that anything that tends to *postpone* or *speed up* combustion can and will have an observable effect on EGT, *even if peak combustion temperatures do not change.* For example, let's say we adjust both magnetos so that ignition occurs earlier than normal—35 degrees before top center, instead of 25 degrees. (Leave everything else the same as before.) Now ignition occurs early, and combustion goes to completion correspondingly early. Instead of peak combustion pressure (and temperature) being reached at, say, 20 degrees after top center, it is now reached 10 degrees after top center. (In reality, it is not a simple one-to-one correspondence—one degree of spark advance doesn't necessarily equal one degree of peak-pressure advance—but for this example we'll keep everything simple.)

What is the effect on EGT? The exhaust valve still opens at the same time—50 degrees before bottom of piston travel. What has happened to the exhaust gases, though, as a result of the premature lightoff of the charge? Assuming detonation did not occur, the expansion/cooloff phase that begins with the reaching of peak combustion pressure and temperature happened 10 degrees earlier than normal; the exhaust gases have been expanding and cooling for 130 degrees of crank travel instead of the usual 120. They will be cooler by the time they reach the EGT probe. Indicated EGT will thus go down.

What happens to CHT in the above example? Ignite the fuel-air charge early, and you give combustion gases a chance to stay longer in the cylinder (they stay for 130 degrees of crankshaft travel instead of 120 degrees), allowing more power to be produced, perhaps, but only at the expense of letting more heat transfer to the cylinder head. CHT goes *up*.

Notice here the absence of any one-to-one correlation between EGT and CHT indications. In fact, in this example the two are *negatively* correlated; one goes up as the other goes down.

What about the reverse situation—retarded timing? Imagine that the magnetos are set to fire *late*. The physical process of combustion can't be rushed; it will go its normal course, requiring something like two or three milliseconds to run its course (the exact time depending on mixture strength and many other factors). Peak pressure will occur late—say at 30 degrees after top center instead of the normal 20. The exhaust valve, again, opens at its normal time (50 degrees before bottom center of piston travel). Because combustion got started late, there is less time for exhaust gases to expand and cool. They are still quite hot when they reach the EGT probe. Indicated EGT goes up. Engine power and CHT both go down slightly.

MAGNETO FAILURE

An interesting case to consider in light of the foregoing discussion is what happens to EGT (and engine power, and CHT) when one magneto is taken off the line, either by mechanical failure or by manually deselecting one or the other mag. If you are beginning to get a feel for the nature of the internal combustion process, you should be able to answer this one on your own, if you think about it long enough.

The important thing to bear in mind here is that flame propagation occurs at a finite rate, and if combustion is started at opposite ends of the combustion chamber by two ignition sources, the event will be of overall shorter duration (shorter by about half) than it would be if only one ignition source were present. In other words, if you take away one spark plug (by shutting down one mag), combustion requires more time to reach completion; the peak-pressure point is shifted late; and exhaust gases have less time to expand and cool before being let out of the cylinder. The gases are hotter than normal when they arrive at the EGT probe. EGT goes up—by a good amount—for all cylinders.

Because the peak-cylinder-pressure point is reached later in the cycle—after the piston has already come partway down on the downstroke—less power is imparted to the crankshaft. Indeed, this is why you have an rpm drop on runup. Cylinder head temperature will go down, but not dramatically. The most dramatic results will come in power (or rpm) and EGT.

SPARK PLUG FOULING

Suppose your EGT for cylinder number four suddenly goes up 75 degrees in flight, but all other cylinders continue to show normal EGT readings. (If the GEM is in Monitor Mode, it will annunciate the excursion by showing you a blinking stack of lights for cylinder number four.) The engine runs smoothly, but you know something has happened in number-four cylinder. What is it?

It could be you've suddenly experiencing spark plug fouling of one plug in number-four cylinder. Perhaps a lead deposit is shorting out the plug's electrodes; maybe the plug (or the ignition lead attached to that plug) has failed outright. This will mimic the mag-failure syndrome described above, except, of course, that it will only affect cylinder number four—not all of the engine's cylinders. With only one functioning spark plug, combustion in the affected cylinder is reaching completion later in the cycle than normal, and exhaust gases are less-expanded/less-cooled by the time the exhaust valve opens. The EGT probe "sees" a hotter exhaust sample for cylinder number four. EGT goes up.

What if the spark plug in question is intermittent? (On some combustion cycles, it fires; on others, it fouls; then it burns clean again and fires, etc.) If the plug spends five minutes not working, then of course EGT will go up a full 75 or 100 degrees, but if the plug fires every other time (for sake of argument), what then? Will EGT go up? Certainly it will. Will it go up 100 degrees? No, because the probe "averages out" the temperature of an alternating hot/cold (or hot/hotter) exhaust stream. The intermittent plug might produce an EGT

The Cessna Skymaster has two engines, four magnetos, 12 cylinders, 24 valves, 24 spark plugs, and 24 ignition leads. Rapidly pinpointing a jug or plug problem without multiprobe EGT is unthinkable in such a plane.

rise of 50 degrees, instead of 75 or 100. Again we see the importance of having a multiprobe EGT system: It is the fact that there is a probe on each exhaust riser that makes diagnosis of a single fouled spark plug possible. With a one-probe system, the EGT effect might go totally unnoticed (unless by stroke of luck the probe is in the riser of the fouling cylinder, of course). And since the cylinder still contains a working spark plug, the engine runs smoothly. The pilot wouldn't notice the fouled spark plug until the next pretakeoff runup—and he or she might not even notice it then.

With the GEM, the fouled-plug problem is annunciated to the pilot in flight the instant it occurs and is identified by cylinder, making maintenance speedier.

INDUCTION SYSTEM
AND FUEL-METERING ANOMALIES

By now you should be thoroughly familiar with the effect of fuel/air ratio on EGT indications, so if we were to ask you what would happen if you were to experience an induction air leak at cylinder number two in flight, your answer should be immediate: "It depends."

It depends how your mixture was set prior to the occurrence of the air leak. (It also depends whether your engine is turbocharged, and operating at high boost—thus blowing air *out* of a leaky connection—or normally aspirated and sucking air *into* a bad connection. We will assume here that the aircraft is normally aspirated, or if turbocharged, operating at low boost.) If you were operating at peak EGT before the blowout, introducing more air to the cylinder can only lower the fuel/air ratio and put the jug on the lean side of peak. EGT would go down accordingly.

If you are operating on the rich side of peak, an induction air leak will cause EGT to go up, for the same reason: The mixture is effectively being shifted lean.

Intake gasket failures are rare. A more common type of "mixture-shift" anomaly is fuel injector nozzle clogging—partial obstruction, in particular. (Total obstruction is less common.) Again, the effect of a fuel restriction—or a lessening of F/A ratio—on the instantaneous EGT indication will depend on whether the cylinder was operating rich of peak, or lean, before the obstruction occurred. But one thing is clear: The affected cylinder will now be operating leaner, all the way across the board. It will be leaner at takeoff, leaner in cruise; leaner on letdown. It may well be your new "leanest cylinder."

The diagnosis of nozzle clogging is often made easier by crossreferencing against a pressure-diaphragm-type (factory) fuel-flow gauge. In airplanes that are so equipped, fuel flow is actually measured in terms of pressure across the nozzles (pressure at the injector manifold). If one or more nozzles begin to clog up, pressure at the injector spider will increase, giving a falsely high fuel-flow indication in the cockpit. The sharp pilot will be able to use this information to verify the presence and location of restricted nozzles.

In a fuel-injected plane, it is important to see that injector nozzles are cleaned once every 100 hours or so, to keep gum and varnish from collecting in nozzle orifices. (Also, dirt has a way of collecting in the air bleed orifice in the side of each nozzle, especially in turbocharged aircraft.) Take note of your cylinder-to-cylinder EGT spread before and after nozzle cleaning. You may be surprised to find that the pattern of EGT readings changes after each nozzle cleaning.

LOSS OF COMPRESSION

Cylinder compression (as measured in the differential compression test) normally wanders up and down considerably over the course of an engine's life. Valves and rings rotate in service, and in different positions they seal differently; also, carbon deposits form on valve faces, then burn off, in service, again affecting compression. Since peak combustion temperatures are related in a very direct way to peak combustion pressures, and since peak pressures are less when valves and rings are allowing gas to escape, periods of low compression have a definite, predictable effect on exhaust gas temperature indications: namely, EGT goes down when compression goes down. Much of your engine's intercylinder EGT spread can be accounted for on this basis.

When something happens to reduce compression drastically—such as piston holing, ring breakage, valve hangup, valve burning, etc.— the effect on EGT is immediate. EGT plummets. (Usually, engine vibration increases at the same time, since the pressure pulses on opposite pistons—normally several tons of force per piston per power event—is no longer in balance.) If you should notice a drop of 100 degrees or more in one or more cylinders, accompanied by noticeable engine vibration, you have ample reason to suspect compression loss in the affected cylinder(s). Land at once and have it checked out.

Incidentally, a prelude to compression loss is often excessive oil consumption (which can affect just one cylinder; it might not affect the engine-as-a-whole in noticeable fashion). If a cylinder is admitting too much oil to the combustion chamber, due to barrel scoring or ring damage, or simple ring or piston wear, the cylinder will "act rich" and run cool, except that the bottom-hole spark plug will tend to collect oil and foul out at low power settings (sometimes even at high power settings), in which case EGT will shoot up 50 to 100 degrees for that cylinder. If both spark plugs from any cylinder appear wet with oil, you're looking at a tipoff to ring or barrel problems. You can expect eventual compression loss, and attendant lowering of EGT.

We might add that when compression has reached a very low point in one or more cylinders, the engine's manifold pressure at idle rpm will be abnormally high (say 18 or 20 inches, rather than 12 or 15) due to the inability of the affected cylinder(s) to draw a strong vacuum.

DETONATION AND PREIGNITION

As you know from the discussion of detonation in the previous chapter, the very essence of detonation is its explosionlike suddenness. It effectively shortcuts the normal combustion process, truncating it from a 2 or 3 or 4-millisecond-long process to something that's all over with in a bang—literally.

Precisely because combustion finishes early, detonation (knock) causes EGT indications to go down. If you are attempting to find peak

EGT—and causing detonation in the attempt—you will notice a broadening and flattening of the EGT curve (Fig. 5-1). In fact, you may not be *able* to find "peak." The peak is no longer a peak. It is a molehill.

When detonation is suspected, CHT should be used as a crosscheck. (It will be elevated.) Conversely, when CHT is running high for no apparent reason, suspect detonation. *Throttle back, enrichen the mixture, and open the cowl flaps—in that order.*

Detonation is more of a threat to turbocharged aircraft than normally aspirated aircraft, and in turbo planes it is more likely to be encountered at high manifold pressures and high altitudes than at lower power settings, or low altitudes. At high altitudes, the turbo compressor is working hard and intake air temperatures are correspondingly high, even though manifold pressures might not be impressive. (Compressor discharge temperature is a function of the *pressure ratio of outgoing versus incoming air.* When your engine is operating at 30 inches of manifold pressure at sea level, the pressure ratio is approximately one. When operating at 30 inches MP at 18,000 feet, the pressure ratio is closer to two—and intake air temperatures are much higher, even though manifold pressure hasn't gone up.)

Detonation can occasionally be a problem for smaller engines if carburetor heat is applied at sea level under full-throttle conditions, although usually there is sufficient "octane margin" in the gasoline to prevent combustion knock if 100LL is being used. Use of automotive gasoline will bring with it a greater risk of detonation. Monitor EGT accordingly. When EGT and CHT diverge—EGT downward, CHT upward, for the engine as a whole—suspect detonation.

Remember that detonation can be a problem for *any* engine when magneto timing has been improperly set, fuel-metering equipment has been maladjusted, etc. Also, the inadvertent use of jet fuel is a popular way of inducing detonation.

Preignition is the natural outcome of prolonged detonation (or of valve overheating, spark plug overheating, deposit buildup, etc.) and has the effect of sending EGT indications all the way to the top of the scale. CHT will also eventually rise, but usually before then the engine self-destructs. Introduction of jet fuel into a reciprocating engine's fuel system is a popular method of causing preignition, as with detonation. Another good way to get preignition going is to use automotive lubricating oils that contain ash-forming detergents. Ash deposits left by such oils glow red in the combustion chamber, setting off combustion well before spark plugs have a chance to fire. Soon thereafter, the engine self-destructs.

Train yourself to have an instantaneous, unflinching response to the first indication of preignition on an EGT gauge: *Reduce power as much as possible, as soon as possible.* Then enrichen mixture, and land.

OTHER ANOMALIES

Occasionally other anomalies come to light. For example, rocker bosses have been known to crack and render valves inoperative. (This results in immediate loss of EGT indication for the cylinder in question, plus considerable engine vibration and power degradation.) Also, deposits can form on valve stems and interfere with the retraction of the valve into the guide on the closing cycle—causing extreme compression loss, moderate engine vibration, power degradation, and low EGT for the jug in question. Episodes of the latter sort have been reported by increasing numbers of Lycoming engine owners in the past five years. Sometimes valves stick in flight; other times (perhaps more commonly) they "cement to the guide" after a hot shutdown. When the owner goes to start the engine for the next flight, the engine shakes and runs poorly until it warms up thoroughly (i.e., the valve loosens), then acts more or less normal. Often, a pushrod bends. Usually, the exhaust valve is involved, and usually just in one cylinder.

In addition to valve problems per se, operators should be on the alert for hydraulic lifter problems. Lifters serve the primary function of removing lash (tolerance buildup) from the valve train at normal operating temperatures. Oil-filled lifters, or tappets, cushion the impact of the cam lobe against the pushrod, and cause the valve to open smoothly, without tapping or pounding. Occasionally, however, lifters become fouled with dirt or varnish and tappet plungers become stuck or collapsed (or bleed down too quickly from advanced wear or improper assembly at overhaul), in which case the function of the lifter is thwarted and tolerances open up in the valve train. In an extreme case, valve opening is delayed (and closing accelerated)—total valve lift is lessened. When this happens with an intake valve, EGT goes down (and CHT goes up)—because fuel and air are admitted with reduced efficiency to the cylinder. Impaired *exhaust-valve* lift, of course, causes CHT to go up (since exhaust gases are retained in the cylinder longer) and EGT to go down (for the same reason).

Operators of Lycoming O-320-H and O-360-E engines should be

especially alert to these symptoms, since cam lobe and lifter spalling/ erosion is a serious problem for many of these engines. If abnormal EGT indications of the foregoing sort are seen in an O-320-H or O-360-E (or TO-360-E), check the oil filter. If it contains metal, check the cam lobes. If they're worn, tear down the engine.

FUEL CONTAMINATION

Contamination of fuel with water has an attention-getting effect on EGT and power output, in that both go immediately to zero. Water isn't the only contaminant that turns up in gasoline nowadays, however. There are also such things to consider as jet-fuel contamination of your fuel tanks (by ill-trained line personnel), accidental use of 80-octane avgas in place of 100, use of automotive gasoline with unanticipated poor octane, and off-spec gasoline (aviation or otherwise) which may have been blended with alcohols of one sort or another. Any of these forms of fuel "contamination" can be detected by EGT analysis.

The accidental introduction of jet fuel (which is essentially kerosene) into a reciprocating engine's fuel has a profound and immediate octane-reducing effect, which for most aircraft simply means immediate, severe detonation on takeoff. (Preignition may or may not follow.) A power loss accompanies detonation, but many, many pilots—some of them quite experienced—have knowingly continued the takeoff roll after experiencing jet-fuel-induced detonation, so the effects are not as obvious as one might suppose. It is a good idea to get in the habit of noticing what your takeoff indications are for EGT and CHT on the various cylinders of your engine. Remember that detonation will have the effect of depressing the exhaust gas temperature (perhaps much more for some cylinders than for others, giving rise to a weird intercylinder spread pattern) while causing a substantial rise in CHT. Also, as stated, some power loss will be evident, and the engine may clatter or make other unusual sounds, or just "be noisy." If preignition is occurring, EGT indications will go offscale-high. Abort the takeoff, if possible; otherwise reduce power and continue flying until a landing can be safely attempted.

The use of any fuel that is too-low in octane (antiknock) quality will result in detonation, whether it is jet fuel, diesel fuel, 80-octane avgas (in an engine designed for 100), low-quality automotive gas, etc. The detonation that results can, however, be light, moderate, or severe in intensity. In some cases, a small reduction in power may make the detonation go away entirely. In other cases, the engine may detonate

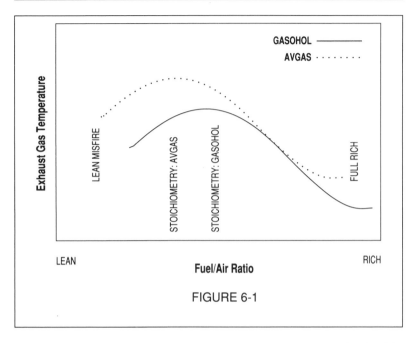

GASOHOL ————
AVGAS ·······

FIGURE 6-1

Alcohol contamination reduces gasoline's latent heat content (hence the height of the EGT curve), and, since oxygen is present in the fuel itself, peak EGT occurs sooner during leanout. (The stoichiometric fuel/air ratio is higher, since less air is needed to burn the partly oxygenated fuel.) As a result, the engine behaves "leaner" than normal.

at idle. (You may be surprised to learn that Research Method octane rating determinations are based on the knock intensity of a test engine running at 600 rpm. The Motor Method is somewhat harsher, and uses 900 rpm as the engine speed.)

Gasoline that has aged in storage may become oxidized, which in practice means it may contain peroxides. Peroxides are unstable molecules of the form X-O-O-Y, where X and Y may be hydrocarbon groups, or hydrogen atoms. The oxygen-oxygen bond that qualifies a peroxide as a peroxide is relatively weak and tends to cause the molecule to want to break in two. Peroxides thus have an extreme octane-reducing (knock-encouraging) effect when added to fuels. The fact that peroxides tend to form spontaneously in fuel that has sat around awhile is what causes fuels to lose octane in storage. The effect is fairly minor, however (fortunately).

A much more important development is the recent trend toward alcohol blending (i.e., mixing of gasoline stocks with methyl, ethyl, or higher alcohols). Various types of alcohols are finding their way into fuels—autogas, primarily, although avgas may also be affected—despite strict government regulations (in the U.S., at least) restricting their use. Alcohols are cheap and high-octane (resistant to knock), and thus attractive as blending agents. The problem with their use is that they are energy-poor. A gallon of isopropyl alcohol yields about 85 percent of the energy value of a gallon of gasoline; a gallon of ethyl alcohol yields about 65 percent as much energy as a gallon gas. Methyl alcohol gives barely *half* the energy of a pound of gasoline. Put any of these in your airplane, and you'll experience a frightening reduction in range.

You'll also experience a frightening change in mixture (EGT) performance. Your carburetor or fuel injector meters fuel on a volume, not a BTU, basis; so for a given air flow, your engine is getting less bang for the fuel-flow buck when alcohol-diluted fuels are used. Not only is the *peak* EGT value *less* than it would otherwise be on straight (undiluted) gasoline, but *peak EGT is reached sooner*. Oxygenated fuels, you'll recall, achieve stoichiometric mixture at a much reduced air/fuel ratio. (You don't have to be a chemist to figure this out.) And alcohols, by definition, are oxygenated. What this means in practice is that with an alcohol-blended fuel, you are already operating much closer to peak EGT, even before you pull the mixture control back (with all that that implies).

In sum: If you find yourself getting less range (or endurance) than planned, with takeoff EGTs higher than they should be but *peak EGTs lower than normal* in cruise (with all cylinders acting leaner than normal), suspect alcohol contamination of your fuel. And change fuel vendors.

These effects are summarized in Fig. 6-1. Note that with alcohol contamination, peak EGT is shifted to the right (to higher fuel/air ratios); in effect, the mixture acts "prematurely lean." But the actual value of peak EGT is *less* than with gasoline, because for a given fuel flow, fewer BTUs are being flowed.

Most hydrocarbon fuels, it turns out, have a lower latent heat (energy) content than gasoline, so generally speaking, any time you find that peak EGT isn't as high as it should be (barring detonation or mechanical malfunctions), you can suspect fuel contamination. Alcohols just happen to be popular contaminants at the moment. Others (such as aldehydes, ketones, arenes, etc.) could just as easily be used.

Unleaded autogas manufactured to ASTM D-439 (the industry

standard for auto fuel) has very nearly the same latent heat content as avgas (about 120,000 BTU per gallon). But autogas doesn't necessarily give the same peak EGT as avgas, even when it is not coblended with alcohols or other oxygenates. The ASTM standards for autogas (D-439) and avgas (D-910) differ significantly with respect to distillation endpoint. Under the current specs, autogas has about a 100-degree (F) *higher* distillation endpoint than 100LL. What this means is that autogas has more "heavy ends"—more high-molecular-weight, high-boiling-point compounds. This doesn't necessarily mean low octane performance; the heavy ends may be of a branched-chain or aromatic configuration (giving good antiknock performance). But heavy ends, by definition, do not volatilize (evaporate) well compared to lighter constituents of gasoline. More of the heavy ends remain in droplet form, rather than vapor form, on their way to the cylinders. They thus contribute less heat energy to the combustion process (a fact that is borne out by the finding of heavy soot deposits in the exhaust pipes and combustion chambers of engines running on autogas). In essence, this means that a smaller fraction of autogas's latent heat energy is usable, at a given mixture ratio, than that of avgas, and peak EGT is lower. (Also, the fuel behaves "leaner.") These effects are more noticeable with some autogas batches and less noticeable with others, since auto fuel production is less tightly controlled than avgas production.

In extremely cold weather, the poor volatilization of autogas heavy ends can become quite apparent, in that the engine may run poorly at wide-open throttle. When this happens, EGT goes down for all cylinders. Some operators have found it necessary to take off on avgas in cold weather, then switch to auto fuel in later cruise flight (see *Light Plane Maintenance*, June 1988, p. 4). Of course, in very warm weather, vapor lock can be a problem, too. Here again, the effect on EGT is dramatic: EGT for all cylinders will vary from high to low, or simply go offscale-low, as vapor lock begins. The usual remedy (consult your POH) is to activate the boost pump and switch tanks.

Chapter 7

EGT INSTALLATION GUIDELINES

Installing an EGT is easy. All EGT manufacturers use basically the same probe technology, so thermocouple installation differs little from EGT to EGT; the same basic considerations apply in all cases. Panel mountings differ, of course, depending on whether the instrument is three inches in diameter or two and a quarter, has one probe lead or many, etc. Even so, the similarities between systems are more numerous than you might think.

The similarities between pilots' and mechanics' *installation mistakes* are also numerous. Typical mistakes include:

1. Siting probes too far away from exhaust ports.

2. Siting probes an unequal distance from exhaust ports (on multi-cylinder installations).

3. Putting probes in slip-joints.

4. Orienting the probe clamp in the wrong direction for screwdriver access.

5. Placing the clamp and probe in needlessly close proximity to nearby objects, such as spark plugs, riser clamps, etc.

Installing an EGT system (especialy a multiprobe system) requires considerable forethought if these and other problems are to be avoided. This chapter should help you avoid many of the most common installation pitfalls, whether you are installing an EGT for the first time or are upgrading your present single-probe system to a more elaborate all-cylinder EGT/CHT system.

INSTALLING EGT PROBES

Siting the probes involves the same considerations no matter what kind of engine you're working with. The idea is simply to locate all EGT thermocouples the same distance away from the exhaust flange, plus or minus a sixteenth of an inch, preferably with each probe well clear of nearby spark plugs and ignition wires, and with the clamp's worm screw in an easy-to-reach position and orientation. Remember

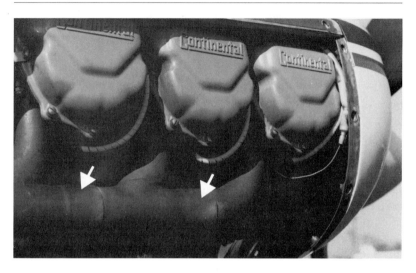

Exhaust slip-joints (arrows) are a bad place to put probes. Joints must be free to move as hot exhaust components expand and contract.

that any time the exhaust pipes have to come off in the future (for top overhaul work, exhaust pipe replacement, or whatever), the probes will have to come off. If you make them easy to take off and put back on, they won't necessitate needless top-overhaul labor surcharges.

Most manufacturers recommend placing EGT probes two inches away from exhaust ports on normally aspirated engines, and four or six inches away from exhaust ports on turbocharged engines. Some years ago, my father and I installed an Insight GEM system on his Enstrom helicopter's Lycoming HIO-360 engine. On two of the HIO-360's risers, there happened to be large exhaust clamps at exactly the four-inch station, so it was a question whether we should go above or below the four-inch mark to locate the EGT probes.

Ultimately, we decided lower was better—all four probes would be installed five inches down from the port. (The important thing is not to mount one probe five inches down from the port, and the other probes four inches down. A probe mounted four inches down will give a higher EGT reading than a probe mounted five inches down, all other things being equal.) We used chalk or soapstone to mark the drilling location on each riser. (Pencil lead should be avoided on exhaust pipes, since it will cause localized carbonization and hot-spotting.)

You'll find that ordinary carbon-steel drill bits aren't best for trying to drill through stainless steel exhaust risers. Plan on making a special trip to the hardware store to buy two cobalt-steel (super hard alloy) drill bits, one 1/8-inch, and one 3/32. You'll use the smaller one for piloting, and the larger one for final drilling.

It's also a good idea to have a very small round file on hand for filing the edges of the holes. Many 1/8 drill bits are actually a couple thousandths' undersize, and to get the probe into the hole may require widening the opening a tiny amount with a file. Once the1/8-in. holes are drilled, it's a simple matter to slip the EGT probes into place and cinch up the band clamps.

Most EGT probes terminate in short wires (four to six inches long) with factory-crimped ring terminals (and screws and nuts) at the ends; these are then hooked up to the harness (the red and yellow wires that go to the cockpit). The harness leads, however, are seldom ready for *immediate* hookup to the probes; it's first necessary to trim the harness leads to proper length, then strip insulation and crimp ring terminals

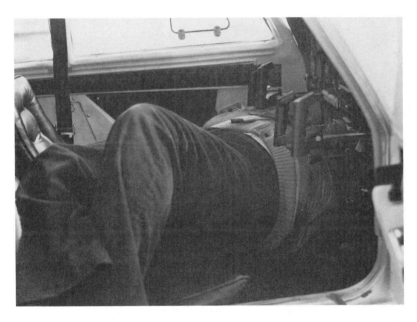

Investigate what's on the other side of the panel before deciding where to put the cockpit display. Often, you'll find unusual doublers, protruding screws or nutplates, or other impediments. Check for adequate hang clearance. The GEM requires 6.285 inches of clear space, plus room for the harness connector.

onto the ends, using hardware provided in the manu-facturer's installation kit.

Note: If you are installing a GEM, the 14-ft harness that comes with the instrument is pre-finished at one end with a harness plug that plugs right into the back of the cockpit display. (The other end of the harness consists of unstrip-ped, unterminated bare wires.) What you need to do before anything else is feed the wires through the firewall,

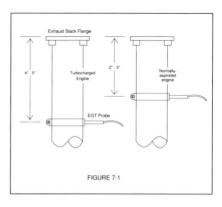

Recommended probe placement for turbo-charged and normally aspirated engines.

leaving enough slack in the harness on the cockpit side so that the wires will reach the instrument without pulling or binding. (Insight does not include spiral-wrap for bunching the harness wires, but it's recommended. Go to the electronics supply store and buy some.)

Two tips: First, you may find it easier to temporarily tape the wires to a "feeler" (such as a coat hanger) and feed them through the firewall that way.

Secondly, look out for high-current wires; you do *not* want low-current thermocouple wires to be bunched with other wires at the firewall crossover, unless those other wires are carrying low current (and thus presenting low chances of electrical interference). When

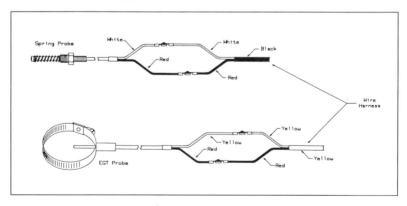

Recommended probe placement for TIT (turbine inlet temp) probe.

you've fed the long ends of the harness wires through the firewall crossover, you can proceed to trim the wires to final length.

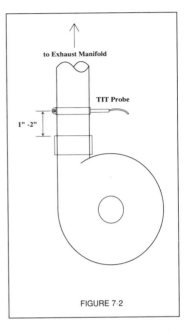

to Exhaust Manifold

TIT Probe

1" -2"

FIGURE 7-2

Trimming the harness leads to final length is easy (you just go at it with a pocket knife). The final length doesn't matter; you can make any lead any length. You'll notice, however, that the EGT probe leads are special thermocouple alloy wires, not just ordinary copper wires. Why? Because of the way a thermocouple circuit works. The hot end of the circuit is called the *hot junction* and the cold end of the circuit is called the *cold junction*. The difference in temperature between the two junctions is what drives the circuit. If you were to heat your cockpit to 1,000 degrees while the EGT was reading 1,400 degrees, the indica-

Recommended probe placement for TIT (turbine inlet temp) probe.

tion on the cockpit EGT would drop to about 400 degrees, because the "cold" junction is no longer so cold. Accordingly, if you were to run copper wires from the probes to the cockpit, the cold junction would begin just outside each exhaust pipe, where the chromel and alumel wires end, and the EGT gauge would read very low. (The temperature difference between the hot and cold ends of the four to six-inch-long alumel/chromel circuit is small in this instance.) In order for an EGT to work properly, the entire wire run from probe to cockpit must be of thermocouple alloy wires. This means, among other things, that you shouldn't try to splice a segment of the wire run (at the firewall crossover, for example) with ordinary copper wire. Use only the appropriate red or yellow *thermocouple wire* to make splices.

Of course, while cockpit temperature changes are never very large, *some* heating and cooling of the panel-mounted EGT gauge (where the cold junction is) occurs, and as a result, EGT indications can wander or be inaccurate unless some sort of compensation is provided in the instrument.

Most EGT manufacturers incorporate a compensation circuit in

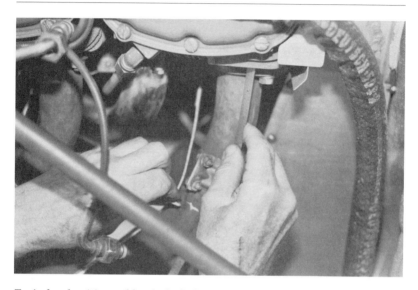

Typical probe-siting problem is the finding of an exhaust clamp on one riser (but not all). Rather than locate one probe lower than the rest, all probes will have to be sited consistent with the "problem probe." Here, the decision was made to site the probe below the clamp, since the engine is turbocharged and a large distance between flange and probe is tolerable. If this had been a normally aspirated engine, the probe should have gone above the clamp. A mark is made with soapstone. (Avoid pencil.)

their gauges. Be sure to ask about this when you are shopping around.

Let's talk more about those thermocouple wires. Notice that if you cut into the yellow Teflon insulation jacket around each EGT lead, you'll see that inside are two insulated wires: a red-insulated wire and a yellow-insulated wire. These are the chromel and alumel thermocouple materials. The cross-section of the small wires is quite tiny, on the order of .035-in. In trimming these wires prior to coupling them to the probe leads, what you need to do is peel back a couple inches of the outer yellow insulation (use a razor; fingernails don't work), then cut the small yellow EGT wire about two inches shorter than the red wire. (The terminals at the probes should be correspondingly staggered. If not, cut your thermocouple leads to the appropriate relative lengths.) Next, you'll strip 3/16-in. of insulation off each lead, and crimp eyelets in place, then bolt the leads to the probes.

For stripping, we recommend the Ideal T-Stripper No. 121 (about $10 from your local electronics outlet), which comes with presized holes for stripping everything up to and including baby carrots. For crimping, Insight Instrument Corp. recommends the AMP 47386 as the "ultimate terminator" (Arnold Schwarznegger notwithstanding).

Insight labels all leads with little numbers (one thru six, for six-cylinder installations). If you are installing a complete EGT/CHT system, you will hook the *yellow* and *red* wires labelled '1' up to the *EGT probe* for cylinder one, and the *black* No. 1 lead to the *CHT probe* on cylinder one, etc. (The TIT lead, should you be installing a GEM 603, is yellow and is unlabelled.) This is so the GEM's bar stacks will correspond to each cylinder in numeric order when read left to right across the display.

Each probe (whether EGT or CHT) has a short pair of wires, staggered in length. On the CHT probes provided by Insight (the probes themselves, not the harness leads), the red wires are longer; on Insight's EGT probes, the red wires are *shorter*. The purpose of this, obviously, is to prevent accidental hookup of the CHT probes to the EGT leads, and vice versa. Even so, it's possible, if you're not paying close attention, to stagger the wires the wrong way, due to careless interpretation of the factory drawings (which are quite clear). Be alert to what you're doing.

Good practice is to perform a pull-test of terminal integrity after crimping any wire. You should be able to pull with 20 pounds of force (or more) on the terminal and not see it slide off in your hand, or even move noticeably. If your crimp fails the test, you'll have to recrimp.

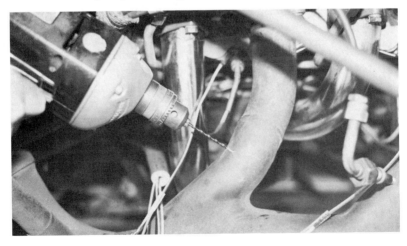

Pilot-drilling for the probe requires the use of a cobalt drill bit (or other specially hardened bit that can cut through stainless steel). A followup pass with a final-size bit will also be made before custom-cleaning the hole with a miniature round file.

Insight provides protective blue thermal sleeves to use over the bolted terminal connections. If your kit doesn't include these sleeves, make some yourself, using high-temp plastic tubing (available at electronics stores). Don't use anything flammable or meltable! And make sure nothing is rubbing against anything when you're all done.

COCKPIT INSTRUMENT INSTALLATION

The Insight Instrument kit contains everything you need to finish the installation (except a drill motor and screwdrivers), including not only the EGT, TIT, and CHT probes, and the 14-ft. wiring harness, but a packet of eyelets, screws, and cable sheaths, copies of the STC documentation, a 40-page user's manual, and a 12-page installation guide with drawings. The wiring harness, as mentioned earlier, is color-coded, with yellow leads for EGT and black leads for CHT.

The first order of business for most owners will be to decide on a panel location for the display. Here, you may find yourself looking at transplanting your 8-day clock to another location, and putting the EGT display in its place; or take existing your existing EGT out and put a GEM in its place. You may also find, after removing the instrument to be swapped out, that there are doubler plates or protruding rivets and screws on the back side of the panel, interfering with gauge relocation. If there are sheetmetal problems behind the panel, it's best

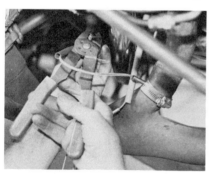

Eyelets must be crimped to the properly trimmed and stripped harness leads before they can be connected to the probe's leads per next photo. Notice that the probe has been clamped in place, with the worm screw facing the outside for easy access. (The probe clamp can be flipped over if necessary to achieve this orientation.)

to discover them before you begin, so take a good look behind the panel. The false front surface of many an instrument panel consists of a single piece of .060-in. plastic, with appropriate cutouts for the instruments. Sandwiched against the underside of the plastic false panel is the "true" panel, consisting, usually, of 0.100-in. 2024-T3 aluminum, with cutouts for the gages. A common problem is that the cutouts in the aluminum don't correspond to the cutouts in the plastic overpanel. It's often the case that a 2.25-in. gauge is mounted in a space originally intended for a 3-inch instrument. Sometimes, moreover, the 3-inch hole on the "aluminum" side is off-center from the 2.25-inch hole in the plastic panel. When you attempt to butt the GEM (or other display) up against the panel from behind, you may find that one or two of its corners are held back by the 3-inch cutout. Or you may find other complications.

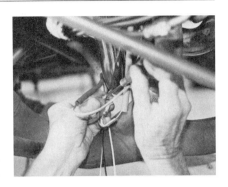

Properly staggered and terminated harness leads can be attached to probe leads via screws. Notice that heat-shield sleeving has been slipped over the wires beforehand.

The message here bears repeating: Don't be surprised to find that others before you have put doubler plates, odd-sized cutouts, etc. on the back of your instrument panel (the real panel, not the false panel), right where you want your new gauge to go. Look behind the panel and see what you've got. It probably won't be what you expected.

The Insight GEM comes with warnings to the effect that panel mounting screws must not penetrate the instrument case more than an eighth of an inch—a stricture that may well force you to custom-cut your own screws to final length with a hacksaw blade. With a 0.100-thick aluminum panel, .060-thick plastic false panel, and 0.125-in. maximum instrument penetration, you're looking at a total of 0.285-in. required thread length (for this example; your panel may be different). To achieve this, you can clamp a pair of half-inch-long screws in a vise and saw their shanks to the proper final length.

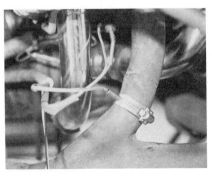

The finished probe installation. The shiny riser is an intake riser. Wires dangling down in front of the exhaust pipe are additional EGT harness wires for adjacent cylinder (which has not been connected yet). CHT wires are visible in upper part of photo.

A pair of 5/32 stainless-steel machine screws, used cantilever-style, may not seem like much, structurally speaking, for securely mounting a 6.3-inch-long instrument. But each screw is good for four pounds of load, and the 12-ounce instrument can be expected to weigh just three pounds under maximum 3.8g flight loading, so two screws—at diagonally opposite corners of the instrument face—gives more than a 100-percent safety factor. Also, the GEM is not wholly cantilevered; it is supported to some degree by the massive cable bundle at the back, which (if you're wise) you'll strap to firm anchor points (with nylon ties) in such a way as to preclude wire-bundle, or instrument, sagging.

CHT PROBES

You may choose someday to upgrade your CHT system to a digital type, or an all-cylinder (multiprobe) system, in which case a few comments on CHT probes are probably in order. First note that cylinder head temperature probes come in several styles, including bayonet- and gasket-type thermocouples and thermistor (or resistive-element-type) probes. If your existing CHT gauge goes dead when you cut the master switch off, you've got the latter type of probe, which is not compatible with the GEM.

This needn't be a problem, however, since Insight doesn't recommend (nor does FAA want) for you to disconnect the existing CHT instrumentation in your plane, if it came from the factory so equipped.

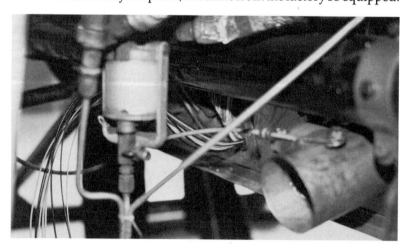

Where EGT/CHT harness wires cross the firewall, there should be no other current-carrying wires nearby. (Interference could result.) A coat hanger or other tool can prove a great help in feeding harness wires through a tight opening one-by-one.

What you want to do is, leave the existing CHT hooked up, and run a gasket-type thermcouple to the spark plug on the affected cylinder, or else use the Insight "adapter probe," which is a little collar-like unit that threads into the cylinder's probe boss and accepts your existing spring-loaded probe. Along the side of the adapter probe (and the reason it's called a "probe") is a J-type thermocouple junction which sends data to the cockpit display. From one and the same cylinder-head boss, it's thus possible to get two CHT readouts (from the factory gage and the GEM). Their indi-

The GEM harness comes factory-ready for plug-in to the cockpit display box. If you've made all the probe connections properly (harness wires are labelled to facilitate this), all you'll have to do is plug the bar connector into the back of the instrument. Two screws hold the harness connector securely to the instrument's aluminum shell.

cations correlate well, too, as it turns out. Before putting the Insight adapter probe into the cylinder head, it's advisable to make another trip to the hardware store for a 3/8-in. thread chaser with which to clean up the probe boss, not only on the cylinder with the factory probe but on all the other cylinders as well. Chasing (cleaning up) the threads makes the work go much easier—as does putting a drop of oil on the probe threads before installing the probes.

A very wide screwdriver is needed to fill the slot in the top of Insight's adapter probe, by the way, but assuming you can round up the right tools, the job goes quickly. The other probe-holders have wrench flats on them, as well as a screwdriver slot; only the adapter probe lacks wrench flats.

GEM INSTALLATION TIPS

If your thermocouple leads have to cross paths with the alternator power wire at any point, be sure to maximize the separation between the wires, and have the thermocouple leads cross the alternator wire at right angles, to eliminate (as much as possible) any electromagnetic couple. Do not bundle the EGT wires in parallel with any current-carrying wire(s).

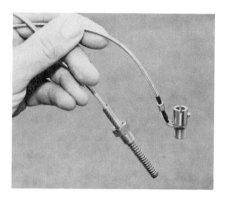

Insight provides two styles of CHT probe: the spring-loaded type (which mounts in pre-existing CHT bosses in each cylinder) and a special adapter probe, which allows simultaneous use of the factory-installed (aircraft manufacturer) CHT bayonet. Spark plug gasket type thermocouples are also available from Insight and will work with the GEM.

You'll find that at the back of the GEM cockpit display, a red wire (harness connector pin 'S') is provided for the main power connection, while a black wire (for pin 15) is intended to go to ground. Insight warns against powering up the instrument while the engine is being cranked over with the starter. Unfortunately, many aircraft do not come with an avionics master switch, which would be the natural solution for this. But an equally good solution suggests itself in the alternator field switch. You can, accordingly, take power off the alternator field switch, and add "alternator: OFF" to your engine-start checklist. That's about it, except for a final visual once-over to deter-

The finished panel installation of the GEM looked like this for Enstrom helicopter N595H. Hole in panel below GEM was later filled by 8-day clock, which was relocated from top to bottom in the course of the installation.

Every aircraft cylinder comes with a CHT boss (not used in most cases). The existing boss usually has corroded or dirty threads. It is good practice to clean up the threads with a thread chaser before installing a CHT probe or adapter.

mine possible areas of chafing, etc. (Use nylon tie-wraps generously to support the harness.) You will need a pair of needle-nose Vise-Grips to get your old CHT bayonet loose, in all likelihood. Also you'll profit by having available a 3/8-in. x 24 UNF thread tap, a wide-slot screwdriver, a wire stripper, a crimping tool, and a length of spiral-wrap abrasion sleeving, not to mention diagonal cutting pliers, miniature wrenches, and the like. If you remember not to accidentally strip the labels off the harness wires, you won't need a continuity tester or ohmmeter, except, possibly, to test the soundness of the ground connection.

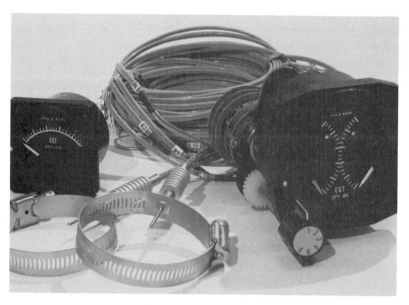

Alcor's switchable "exhaust analyzer" (at right) was state-of-the-art 20 years ago when it supplanted the single-probe Ekonomix gauge (also at one time state-of-the-art). Owners now have much more to choose from.

Chapter 8

EGT ERGONOMICS

Ergonomics refers to what the computer programmer would call the "user interface"; it's how good a fit there is (or isn't) between the device and the human being using the device. An appliance that is instinctively easy to use is said to have good ergonomics. The question of ergonomics is an all-important one when it comes to EGT systems, because the amount of data that can be conveyed by an all-cylinder EGT/CHT/TIT system is impressive, and unless that data can be presented in a clear, intelligible form, it's useless. Anybody in the market for an EGT system—or a system upgrade—would do well to think long and hard about EGT ergonomics, because in the EGT field, as in the computer field, it's the user interface that counts.

As in computers, a design revolution has taken place in EGTs in recent years, partly because of the availability of different display technologies (LED, liquid crystal, etc.) and partly because of the increasing demand by pilots for better, more accurate, more all-encompassing engine instrumentation. Where at one time, all exhaust gas temperature gauges were of the analog single-needle type, today the aircraft owner can choose from a bewilderingly diverse variety of setups, including:

1. Multiple-probe, single-needle analog EGT, switchable. (Alcor.)

2. Multiple-probe, multiple-needle analog EGT. (Alcor, KS Avionics.)

3. Multiple-probe EGT & CHT, analog display, switchable by mode and by cylinder. (KS Avionics.)

4. Single-probe EGT, single-probe CHT, plus oil temperature, LCD display, switchable by mode. (Electronics International.)

5. Single-probe liquid-crystal digital EGT. (Electronics International.)

6. Single-probe LCD-type EGT and CHT, switchable by mode. (Electronics International.)

7. Multiple-probe LCD-type EGT, switchable by cylinder. (Electronics Intl., KS Avionics.)

8. Multiple-probe LCD-type CHT, switchable by cylinder. (Electronics Intl., KS Avionics.)

9. Multiengine version of the above, switchable by engine. (Electronics Intl.)

10. Multiprobe LED-type numeric-display, scanning. (JP Instruments)

11. Multiprobe LCD-type numeric-display, scanning. (Electronics International.)

12. Multiple-probe EGT/CHT (with or without TIT), plasma-discharge bar-graph display. (Insight GEM).

The central question facing the owner who wishes to upgrade is: Which of these systems is best, not only from the standpoint of efficient utilization of panel space and most-features-for-dollars-spent, but simple ergonomics?

SWITCHABLE MULTICHANNEL SYSTEMS

The cheapest and simplest upgrade option, of course, is to add probes to each cylinder and put a selectable (switchable) display on the panel, giving your existing single-needle or single-LCD gauge multichannel capability. Switchable systems continue to be popular, despite the trend toward fancier all-in-one displays, simply because they *are* low-cost and easy to install, while making economical use of panel space. There are serious drawbacks to the switchable-display (read one cylinder at a time) setup, however. Adding a selector knob may give you access to more information about your cylinders, but you're still limited to observing one cylinder at a time. To put it differently, you're *ignoring* 75 percent of your cylinders 100 percent of the time, in a four-cylinder installation, or 83 percent of your cylinders 100 percent of the time, in a six-cylinder engine.

Crosschecking cylinders with a switchable EGT requires not only excellent short-term memory, but spare hands to flip the switch and lean the mixture. Also, finding the leanest cylinder (not the *hottest* cylinder, remember, but the *leanest*) takes a good deal of time, and once the mixture has been set, inflight trend monitoring is difficult unless you fiddle constantly with the selector knob.

Doing this on instruments is unthinkable without an autopilot (or copilot). VFR is another matter, of course, but it's still no fun to try remembering temperature trajectories for all cylinders as you switch through them one at a time during leanout. (And since the leanest cylinder can change from day to day, it's no use thinking you can leave the selector set for the leanest cylinder, and just lean by reference to a particular cylinder on each flight. That cylinder may not be the one you want when you get into the plane tomorrow.)

The term "exhaust analyzer", as applied to switchable systems, is actually something of a misnomer, inasmuch as such systems actually analyze nothing. It's the *pilot* who analyzes, switching back and forth between cylinders, memorizing numbers or needle positions, figuring temperature trends over time, and coming up with a clear picture of the engine's operational status (perhaps while performing an IFR scan and talking to ATC). Troubleshooting in this situation is difficult, and often an after-the-fact exercise: Once a cylinder is dead, you can switch through the cylinders and isolate the cold EGT probe quickly. But when it comes to spotting *intermittent* problems, you have to hope the

Switchable mono-displays offer an economical upgrade to single-probe systems, since the original cockpit display unit can often be kept in place and a selector switch added in modular fashion. Such a setup offers the pilot a good deal more information than a single-probe system. But it's up to the pilot to remember EGT readings as he scans through the cylinders.

problem occurs on the presently-selected jug, since if it occurs on a non-selected cylinder, you may *never* see it.

Switching switches and performing mental arithmetic is part of flying, but that doesn't mean you want to make engine monitoring any more difficult than it has to be. Switchable EGTs are tedious to use effectively. Also, they tend to hide information from the pilot; you have to go out of your way to see all the available information. For these reasons, many owners of switchable exhaust analyzers make it a practice simply to leave the selector knob on one cylinder—usually what they believe to be the "leanest cylinder"—from flight to flight, rotating the knob *only* when trouble is suspected. There are a couple of serious problems with this approach. First, the leanest cylinder can change at any time. (A change in ring rotation, a drift in cylinder compression, or a piece of dirt under a valve is all it takes.) Secondly, the lack of ability to see intercylinder EGT *trends* makes it dfifficult to spot developing engine problems *before* they become serious—which is one of the main reasons to have a multichannel "exhaust analyzer" in the first place.

The bottom line is this: To get the most out of an EGT system, you have to be able to discern *trends*. Cruise leaning is done by reference to peak EGT, for example, and peak EGT can *only* be determined by trend information. (The actual numerical value of peak EGT, in degrees Fahrenheit, will vary from cylinder to cylinder and day to day; that's less important than *where the needle peaks*, in relation to fuel flow or mixture position. That's a dynamic observation.) Trend monitoring is also the key to troubleshooting via EGT/CHT. Only by noting *changes* in intercylinder temperature patterns can you get an early warning of impending trouble, whether it's minor (for example, plug fouling, induction air leak, injector nozzle gumming) or major (valve sticking, broken rings, holed piston). There's no way a pilot can get a jump on trouble if he or she can't *spot* and *track* temperature variations *as they are occurring.*

After a failure has occurred, of course, a switchable multichannel EGT will allow the pilot to isolate the failure to the affected cylinder— which is more than the owner of a single-probe system can do. But the ability to point to a broken cylinder after it breaks is nowhere near as important as the ability to spot mechanical problems *before* they occur—or at least, before they become a threat to inflight safety.

DIGITAL VS. ANALOG DISPLAY

LCD (liquid crystal display) and LED (light emitting diode) EGT gauges have been available for ten years or more from such well-known suppliers as Electronics International, KS Avionics, and (more recently) JP Instruments. Certainly, if one-degree accuracy were important for leaning an engine, a digital readout would be extremely useful, even essential. But as it turns out, one-degree accuracy is *not* necessary—or even desirable—in an EGT system, *unless* a turbo-charger is present in the exhaust (or the engine is apt to develop EGTs beyond 1,600 degrees).

For most operators, a one-degree change in EGT simply isn't of practical importance in leaning or troubleshooting.

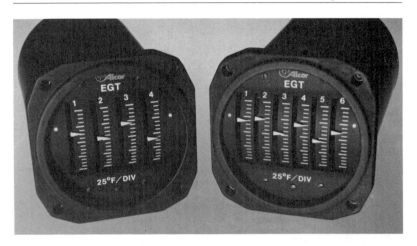

Alcor's multidisplay heads offer the pilot an easily assimilated picture of combustion status in each cylinder. Intercylinder EGT spread is easily discerned, and developing trends that might be easy to miss on a switchable mono-display are readily spotted on the all-cylinder readout (provided the pilot has his or her eye on the gauge, of course). The analog readouts give essential infinite resolution, mooting the "resolution coarseness" or "gauge accuracy" issue. For a non-CHT/non-TIT instrument, the Alcor multidisplay rates very high for ergonomics. It does everything one could ask of a direct-reading analog unit.

Some types of data are best represented numerically; others are best represented in analog fashion. Most of us prefer to see airspeed displayed on an analog gauge with a needle that moves clockwise around a dial. Most of us prefer to see radio frequencies represented digitally (numerically), rather than via an analog scale (as on the old Narco Omnigator). In still other instances—as with a magnetic compass—we prefer to see both numbers *and* an infinitely sliding scale. If *all* cockpit indications—not just EGT and CHT, but airspeed, altitude, rate of climb, heading, VOR bearing, ammeter load, etc.—were displayed in strictly numeric form, the pilot could never assimilate the data; it would be instant information overload. (Note, though, that the *amount* of information hasn't changed—only the presentation.)

The same argument applies to EGT. It's not surprising, when you think about it, that no one has yet come out with a simultaneous, all-cylinder display of EGT in *liquid-crystal numerals*. All multichannel EGTs that use a straight numeric presentation tend to be of the switchable, one-cylinder-at-a-time variety (with all the drawbacks in terms of high pilot workload, difficulty of trend monitoring, etc., that that entails). The primary usefulness of EGT is as a trend phenomenon. Thus, an analog presentation makes sense. Other presentations of the data can be used, of course, but most pilots won't be able to *interpret* trend data as readily with pure-numeric displays.

A purely numeric display makes sense for such things as fuel quantity (where extreme accuracy is important), TIT (for which there are definite go/no-go limits), fuel flow, etc. But for something as dynamic as EGT—where the individual numbers change often (and mean nothing out of context)—an analog approach is hard to beat. If you *don't mind* flipping back and forth between cylinders in flight, constantly comparing numbers and mentally calculating intercylinder EGT spreads (as well as EGT *trends*) to arrive at a determination of leanest cylinder versus richest—and if you *don't mind* troubleshooting gummed injector nozzles, drifting mag timing, or other

KSA's Hexad II multidisplay is a top-of-the-line alternative to Alcor's popular (and expensive) EGT-only units, incorporating a flipflop switch for toggling CHT and EGT modes. Unlike the Alcor counterparts, the KSA units have an expandable scale: Adjustment of the tiny knobs along the bottom of the gauge will allow the instrument to display EGTs over a 900-to-1,800 degree range. (The knobs can also be used to zero out the pointers in flight.) A CHT overtemp event will cause the light at the upper right to come on and stay on; a shock-cooling event will cause the light to pulse. (The annunciating thresholds are user-settable.) Although the visual design of the Hexad II is a bit on the busy side, the unit's capabilities are formidable, combining the infinite resolution of analog meters with all-cylinder CHT and over/undertemp annunciation.

problems, while watching the numbers flicker as you adjust power or mixture—then simply upgrading to a switchable LCD-type EGT may well be acceptable. Most pilots probably do not need the extra data-interpretation workload, however.

SCANNING DEVICES

Police radio and CB (citizen's band) transceiver manufacturers were quick to realize the importance of being able to free up a driver's hands by incorporating *automatic scanning* as a feature in their products. Recently, a couple of EGT makers, recognizing the desirability to

The JP Instruments Scanner is essentially a switchable mono-display (LED-type) instrument that eliminates the chore of manually switching between cylinders (although a manual mode switch on the front can enable that feature, if the pilot desires). Later versions of the instrument incorporate overtemp annunciation.

keeping a pilot's hands free, have come up with "channel scanning" exhaust analyzers. (Again, the term "exhaust analyzer" is not to be taken too literally; the pilot is the one doing the analyzing.) These devices allow the pilot to see all cylinders' EGT readouts *in sequence,* automatically, without the need for removing hands from the controls. J.P. Instruments of Huntington Beach, California offers scanning-type EGT/CHT systems (with both EGT and CHT combined into one 2-1/4 inch panel display), starting at under $1,000 for a four-cylinder EGT-only system. (Six-, seven-, eight-, and nine-cylinder models are available on request.) Electronics International, Inc. has also entered the "scanning-EGT" market with a device that flashes EGT numerically on an LCD gauge.

JPI's instruments have a *manual mode* in which the pilot can linger on one cylinder *or* step through the cylinders by pushing a button, as well as an *automatic* mode in which the LED-type display flashes the EGT (or CHT) for each cylinder in sequence, at the rate of 4 to 5 seconds per cylinder readout. (It takes 20 seconds or so to cycle through all six EGT readouts for an IO-520.) Electronics International's latest gauges offer similar features. Display resolution on the JPI instrument, however, is plus-or-minus 10 degrees, whereas Electronics International's displays read actual degrees Fahrenheit to one-degree accuracy.

JPI has recently expanded its instrument capability (as Electronics International also has) to include annunciation of EGT and/or CHT overtemp excursions. "Annunciation" doesn't mean that a bell goes off; it means that the display stops scanning when an overtemping jug is encountered. It is still up to the pilot to be alert enough to notice that the gauge has stopped scanning. But at least the instrument does the work of "remembering" that an overtemp occurred, and which cylinder was involved. If the pilot was too busy talking to ATC or flying the plane to notice the temperature excursion, it will still be possible for the pilot to see later (at his or her leisure) whether or not an overtemp event has taken (or is taking) place, since the no-longer-scanning display has "flagged" the errant jug.

Certainly the scanning EGTs represent a step in the right direction, because they truly do reduce pilot workload. But the thorny problem of information assimilation remains. The question that every pilot who is considering buying one of these gauges should ask himself (or herself) is: How can a busy aviator *absorb and remember* EGT/CHT data as an instrument flashes sequences of numbers? How can long-term *trends* be discerned? More than that, how can the *leanest cylinder* (not the hottest cylinder) be found with such a device? (We don't mean to imply that it cannot be done; it can. You need to enter the manual mode, set the gauge for cylinder number one, begin leaning, determine where peak EGT occurs *as a function of fuel flow or mixture position*, then repeat the foregoing process for each cylinder consecutively; then compare peak-EGT fuel flows or mixture positions for each cylinder to determine the leanest cylinder—i.e., the cylinder that achieved peak EGT at the richest mixture position or highest overall engine fuel flow.) How would a busy IFR pilot fit a scanner's nominal 30-second duty cycle into a normal IFR panel scan? Even assuming it can be done, the question arises whether the scanning feature makes *troubleshooting* any easier (except in the case of a totally dead cylinder). The scanning EGTs are best thought of as single-readout switchable EGTs. (In manual mode, that's all they really are.) They take the "work" out of using the selector switch. The newer gauges also take the work out of finding an overtemping jug. But in "scan mode," it is still up to the pilot to monitor the cylinder readouts, observe trends, mentally calculate EGT spreads, and formulate a coherent picture of engine operational status.

The scanning EGTs (particularly those models that have an "overtemp flag" feature) are without a doubt an improvement on manually switchable EGTs, and many plane-owners will like the novel presentation of data. (Those who tire of squinting at low-brightness LCD readouts will appreciate JPI's bright-red LEDs.) But once the novelty wears off, from a *troubleshooting* standpoint—or even for finding an engine's leanest cylinder—a scanner is functionally little different than a switchable EGT. It is still *hiding* 75% or more of the data 100% of the time.

ALL-CYLINDER DISPLAYS: ANALOG

To a large extent, the ergonomic shortcomings of the "switchable digitals" have been overcome in the analog-style all-cylinder EGTs manufactured by Alcor and KS Avionics. Alcor's vertical-readout multineedle displays show EGT only (switchable by engine, for twins)—no CHT, at present—and start at about $2,000 for a four-cylinder kit with probes and harness. KS Avionics' vertical-readout gauges indicate EGT *or* EGT/CHT (switchable by mode) and can be ordered with an overtemp annunciation option. (The CHT overtemp light will come on at any pilot-set temperature.) KSA's Tetra A four-cylinder EGT with overtemp alarms for each cylinder lists at approximately $950 (with probes). TIT is not an option in the Alcor system or the KSA instruments, unless the owner specially wires one of the EGT probes to a TIT mounting location; but even then, calibration is the owner's responsibility.

Neither Alcor nor KSA vertical-readout systems comes with numbered scales. (Scale divisions, however, are provided, representing 25 degrees Fahrenheit per hash mark in each case.) The lowest indication on the Alcor instrument corresponds to about 1,300 degrees. For many planes, this means there will be no needle movement on runup (and certainly none at idle). KSA's gauges, on the other hand, have an expandable scale: By adjusting tiny control knobs at the bottoms of the meters, the gauge's pointers can be made to indicate across a range from 900 to 1,800 degrees F, making runup diagnostics possible.

The author flew a normally aspirated Piper Seminole containing the Alcor multineedle gauge and had a chance to "get to know" the Alcor gauge quite thoroughly on a coast-to-coast flight from Bridgeport, Connecticut to Los Angeles, California. One can go crazy calibrating the Alcor unit on installation (it's filled with trim pots), but assuming it is set up properly to begin with, it is an easy unit to use and does everything you'd expect a non-annunciating all-cylinder EGT to do, except provide midscale indications during the mag check. (Two needles came off their pegs, barely, during runup at 1,700 rpm. For the gauge to be useful in runup, the pretakeoff mag check would have to be done at close to 2,200 rpm.) Response time for the Alcor unit is quick—well within the needs of a human pilot—and the display (larger than most, at 3-1/8 inch across) is easy to read at a glance, permitting a rapid assessment of intercylinder EGT spreads in flight. In addition, the unit the author flew with in the Seminole was of the switchable left-engine/right-engine (left-right flipflop) kind, which was a tremendous panel-space-saver. (In a twin, the high list price of the Alcor multidisplay is quickly rendered a non-issue when compared with the prospect of paying for two GEMs, say.) For an EGT-only type gauge (with no TIT or CHT capability, and no annunciation features), the Alcor unit is exceptional, and a very attractive buy for twin-owners (in the absence of a left-right flipflop GEM).

KSA's Tetra and Hexad (4- and 6-cylinder) EGT/CHT systems operate in similar fashion to Alcor's multidisplays, with a few important differences. One difference is, CHT can be shown on the same gauge at the flick of a mode switch (not possible with the Alcor unit); this feature puts the KSA unit in a class by itself. Secondly, various types of annunciation are available on KSA's gauges, including EGT overtemp (by cylinder), TIT overtemp, CHT overtemp, and CHT shock cooling (user-settable to any cooldown-rate threshold). Probably the biggest difference between KSA's vertical-readout EGTs and Alcor's is the pointer-alignment feature. At the bottom of each meter is a dial, the purpose of which is to allow the pilot to adjust the indicator needle to any desired height on the scale. According to KSA's Bill Simpkinson, this allows the pilot to expand the useful range of the instrument (which has a nominal 250-degree peg-to-peg scale), and also, if the pilot wishes, line up all pointers in cruise (after final leaning), for purposes of making subsequent EGT excursions immediately apparent.

At first, the notion of being able to "zero out" the intercylinder EGT spread (to facilitate inflight troubleshooting) sounds eminently reasonable. But many experts feel it is better to be able to see the day-to-day pattern of peaks and dips in EGTs between cylinders. This is a matter of individual taste, in the end. However, a case can be made for *not* zeroing out the EGT spread, since it's often useful to know what the EGT spread is from hottest cylinder to coolest, on a minute-by-minute basis during a long flight (especially when injector nozzle problems are suspected). If you keep zeroing out the pointers (the argument is made), you *may* lose sight of what's normal, and what's not, for the various cylinders. You might zero out a bonafide problem. (Bill Simpkinson doesn't agree with this; he points out that it is possible, at any time, to return the pointers to their original staggered locations, thus setting the gauge up for viewing EGT "spread." I really don't wish to disagree with him. I merely want to point out to the reader that there are two sides to the "zeroing out" argument.)

Of course, it *is* nice to be able to lean an engine *almost* to peak, then quickly zero out the needles (lining them up in a neat row), then continue leaning until one pointer suddenly drops—revealing (presto!) the leanest jug. But whether this ability is really paramount is up to the individual. Finding the leanest cylinder with Alcor's gauge is no particular problem, so it's hard to give KSA's product the nod strictly on the basis of its having zeroable pointers.

KSA's gauges display more information (CHT as well as EGT) and provide more features (overtemp annunciation, for example) than the Alcor units. After looking at both, I

Insight's GEM 602 displays EGT as orange bar stacks (25 degrees per bar); a non-illuminated bar marks the CHT for each cylinder (calibrated in hundreds of degrees along the right egde of the display). CHT resolution is also 25 degrees per bar. Unlike other EGT systems, the GEM incorporates an onboard microprocessor programmed to find the leanest cylinder (in Lean Mode) and annunciation overtemp events (in Monitor Mode). EGT scale is non-linear at the low range, to allow EGT observations on pretakeoff runup.

can truthfully say I only wish an Alcor gauge were available with EGT *and* CHT information on the same dial. Alcor is to be commended, however, for outpacing some of its competitors in one regard: Its multidisplay head comes in a twin-engine version as well as a single-engine version. (KSA can supply this also.) In the Seminole that yours truly flew, it was a simple matter to switch back and forth from engine to engine and see the intercylinder EGT spread for each engine, at a glance.

ALL-CYLINDER DISPLAYS: DIGITAL

The Main Contender in the all-cylinder vertical-readout EGT/CHT arena is the Graphic Engine Monitor, manufactured by Insight Instrument Corporation. Certainly, no other engine instrument appearing in the last 10 years has had as profound an effect on the market as the GEM (which has set a new standard for all-cylinder EGT displays, and for excellence of engineering). Unfortunately, no other EGT instrument is as widely misunderstood (or as underappreciated) as the GEM. There's much more going on here than meets the bifocals.

The Graphic Engine Monitor is truly that: an engine monitor. It displays EGT, CHT, and TIT information all at once, continuously, on one 2-1/4 inch panel display, and is at this writing the *only* instrument on the market that does so. (Others flip-flop between modes.) EGT is displayed as columns of bright orange bars, one column per cylinder, with one bar for each 25 degrees of EGT, Fahrenheit. Cylinder head temp is displayed as a *non*-illuminated (dark) bar within each field of orange bars. The CHT scale is calibrated, with markings for 300, 400, and 500 degrees F shown on the right side of the display. EGT is not referenced to a degree scale as such, but TIT (in the Model 603) is depicted as a numeric readout at the top of the gauge, accurate to within 10 degrees. (Note that the actual readout is only three digits long. Insight drops the fourth digit in the TIT number; it's up to the user ot add a zero to the end of the number.)

The GEM scale (for EGT) is not simply linear from top to bottom. Instead, an expanded scale allows the GEM to display EGT at temperatures as low as 800 degrees Fahrenheit, making taxi and runup diagnostics possible. In addition to installing a Model 603 GEM in an Enstrom helicopter (see Chapter 8), your author flew a normally aspirated 1977 Piper Lance equipped with a Graphic Engine Monitor (wired for both EGT and CHT). As advertised in Insight's literature, the unit's display began "stacking bars" mere seconds after engine start, with CHT clearly readable by the time the runup area was reached. During the runup, each EGT readout grew taller by one bar on single-mag operation (which is normal; EGT is hotter operating on a single mag). A brief check of the mixture control shows it is possible to get a large (five or six-bar) rise in EGT even at as little as 1,700 rpm.

In flight, the GEM has two modes of operation. (See Chapter 7 for a complete rundown of how to use the GEM.) The *lean mode* is selected by pushing the tiny mode button and holding it in for about two seconds, which makes the orange "EGT" letters start flashing in the upper left portion of the display. At this point, the pilot begins coming back on the mixture lever. The EGT bar-stacks rise accordingly; meanwhile, the GEM's Intel 8048 microprocessor—which is tracking the EGT rise for each cylinder as a function of time (and *comparing*

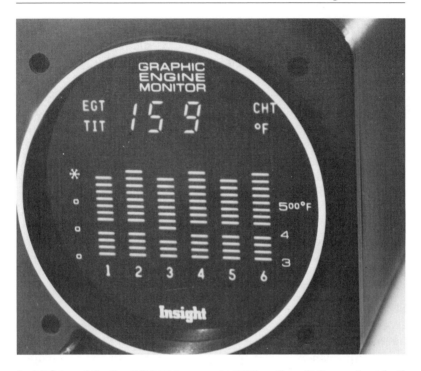

Insight's top-of-the-line GEM 603 incorporates TIT (as a three-digit numeric readout) as well as fulltime (not flipflop) all-cylinder EGT and CHT. The TIT display resolution is ten degrees Fahrenheit; Insight omits the fourth digit. Price is approximately $2,000, including probes and harness.

cylinders with each other)—determines which of the engine's cylinders is leanest *and*—at the same time—begins flashing the appropriate stack of bars as that jug approaches peak. (On the Lance, it happened to be the number three cylinder.)

When the bar stack for the leanest cylinder starts flashing, the pilot can punch the mode button to stop the flashing, thus entering the *monitor mode.* At this point, the operator can either keep the mixture control where it is—namely, at peak EGT on the leanest cylinder—or enrichen as desired for cruise. In Monitor Mode, the GEM displays realtime EGT continuously *and* monitors all cylinders for EGT excursions. If any EGT, for any cylinder, increases by more than 50 degrees, that cylinder's bar-stack will begin flashing and *keep on* flashing until the pilot hits the reset button. Intermittent problems, such as a fouled spark plug, are revealed in clear fashion this way, so that even if the pilot is busy in the cockpit and doesn't happen to be looking at the EGT when the problem happens, he or she can still know about it later, because when the pilot looks up (even five minutes later—or a half hour), the bar-stack will be flashing.

The GEM's critics carp about the instrument's 25-degree resolution, noting that a 10-degree change in EGT (or CHT) can go undisplayed. But Insight's John Youngquist, designer of the GEM (and himself a Bonanza owner), responds by asking: "How much display accuracy do you *really* need? I mean, if you had *tenth*-of-a-degree display accuracy, would it let you lean your engine any better? Could you *troubleshoot* your engine better?" Youngquist conducted flight tests of prototype GEMs with 10-degree and 15-degree resolution, and found, to his consternation, that the display jumped around quite a bit—the data changed too rapidly. The GEM's 25-degree resolution was arrived at empirically; Youngquist decided on it after trying finer resolutions.

The GEM's computer brain, of course, actually senses and tracks EGT with fraction-of-a-degree accuracy. The fact that the *display* accuracy happens to be 25 degrees doesn't mean the instrument's internal accuracy is that coarse. Far from it. The GEM display represents a true clean-sheet-of-paper attempt at ergonomic design. It does not attempt to imitate other approaches; it attempts to display EGT information in the most contextually appropriate manner possible.

Considering the GEM's ease of use/interpretation, its annunciation features, and its ability to display CHT, EGT, and TIT all at once, the near-$2,000 list price of the Model 603 GEM (including probes) is not unreasonable. It packs a lot of capability into a very compact package. Light twin owners, unfortunately, must (at present) find panel space—and the pecuniary wherewithal—to buy *two* GEMs, since Insight does not offer a switchable left-right gauge. This situation may soon be rectified, however.

In the end, the choice of single-probe versus switchable, analog multidisplay versus digital, scanning versus non-scanning, and multi-CHT versus single-CHT systems lies with the end-user. The high-end units with simultaneous all-cylinder readouts may seem costly (and are, if you own a twin), but when a serious engine problem arises, the ease of troubleshooting provided by a high-end unit quickly causes most owners to forget about what it cost to install the system. In the air, when trouble starts, especially, *more* information is better. For this reason, every owner of a single-probe EGT system ought to consider upgrading to a multi-probe system as soon as possible—before prices go up further.

Appendix A

MANUFACTURERS

Alcor, Inc., 10130 Jones-Maltsberger Road, San Antonio, TX 78284 (phone 1-800-354-7233; in Texas, 1-800-348-3835).

Electronics International, Inc., 5289 N.E. Elam Young Parkway, Hillsboro, OR 97124 (phone 503/640-9797).

Insight Instrument Corp., Box 194, Ellicott Station, Buffalo, NY 14205 (phone 716/852-3217 or 416/871-0733).

J.P. Instruments, P.O. Box 7033, Huntington Beach, CA 92615 (phone 714/962-0112).

KS Avionics, Inc., 25216 Cypress Ave., Hayward, CA 94544 (phone 415/785-9407).

Appendix B

THE GRAPHIC ENGINE MONITOR IN OPERATION

The Insight Instrument Corp. Graphic Engine Monitor represents such a radical departure from typical EGT systems—and such a popular success, as well—that no book of this kind would be complete without a separate section devoted to it. With the introduction of the GEM in 1981, EGT technology truly came into the Computer Age. The GEM's onboard Intel 8048 microprocessor and novel cockpit display (involving stacks of orange plasma-discharge lights) make it unique among high-end EGT/CHT systems—and also one of the most expensive, at $2,000-and-change. But the GEM is more than just a sexy display wired to Stone-Age-technology thermocouples. It incorporates a plethora of sophisticated, software-driven features that are by no means obvious to the untrained observer. The GEM is more than an EGT: It is a device for finding the leanest cylinder of an engine; it annunciates EGT excursions in cruise; it reads CHT fulltime, as well as EGT; it displays information in a way that is readily understandable to the pilot; and on top of everything else, it is self-calibrating (and incorporates a self-diagnostic test mode).

The GEM has often been criticized (by its competitors, mainly) for having a "coarse resolution"—i.e., the bar-graph display reads EGT only in 25-deg. F increments, rather than 10-degree or single-degree increments. Inherent in this sort of criticism is a misunderstanding of the fundamental purpose of EGT systems. As explained further in the chapter on EGT ergonomics, there is no need to see one-degree (or even 10-degree) changes in EGT; nor is there a need—unless you're flying a turbocharged aircraft—to be able to read EGT in actual degrees Fahrenheit or Celsius. Unless you're operating above 1,650 F, the absolute temperature of your exhaust is of no concern for leaning or troubleshooting. What the pilot mainly needs to be able to see are EGT *trends*, cylinder-to-cylinder and moment-to-moment. The GEM adequately addresses this need. Rather than deluging the pilot with an overabundance of numeric data (temperatures for all cylinders' EGT and CHT), the GEM merely presents a picture of the overall state of heat flow throughout the engine. Insignificant changes in temperature (one-degree changes in EGT, for example) are not displayed. Significant changes (25 degrees or more) register instantly. A minimum of pilot interpretation/interpolation is required.

If you already own a GEM system, you are no doubt fully versed in its use and you are justified in skipping this chapter. If you are thinking of buying a GEM, or are merely curious as to how the GEM works in day-to-day operation, read on and you'll discover just how different an animal the Graphic Engine Monitor is.

BASIC MODES OF OPERATION

The Graphic Engine Monitor has three basic modes of operation: Test Mode, Lean Mode, and Monitor Mode.

Test Mode offers a self-diagnostic test routine for the pilot or installer to use when checking the functioning of the instrument. To activate the Test Mode, begin with electrical power off, then hold the reset button down while powering up the instrument. The GEM will go through a precisely programmed test pattern, for as long as you hold the reset button in. Starting with display column number one (all the way to the left), orange bars will "stack up" until the full column is illuminated, then blank out; then column two will light up, and each column will light up in succession. The test will end with column six, or repeat as long as the reset button is depressed. (It is not necessary for the pilot to invoke Test Mode at the beginning of every flight. The Test Mode is designed to be used by the repair technician, when trouble with the system is suspected.)

Lean Mode is used when setting the mixture for cruise, or any time it is necessary to identify the engine's leanest cylinder. This mode can be entered at any time by holding the reset button down for about two seconds, until the EGT annunciator in the upper left corner of the display flashes. (The reset button can then be released.) When the instrument is in the Lean Mode, it waits for the pilot to begin leaning the mixture; and when the mixture is leaned, the GEM's computer analyzes the EGT outputs of all four (or all six) thermocouple probes to arrive at a determination of the leanest cylinder. The lean cylinder is then annunciated to the pilot via a flashing column corresponding to the EGT readout of the cylinder in question. As explained further below, Lean Mode is used during the final fine-tuning of the mixture.

Monitor Mode (identified by the steady illumination of the EGT annunciator in the upper left corner of the display) may entered or re-entered at any time by simply pushing the reset button briefly. (If the reset button is held too long, then Lean Mode will be activated; see above.) Each time the Monitor Mode is entered, any blinking columns will stop flashing, and current EGT readings are automatically stored in computer memory for comparison to future readings. Should *any* cylinder's exhaust gas temperature rise 50 degrees or more (from now till the end of the flight), the corresponding column will start blinking, signifying a change in combustion dynamics.

Note that with the GEM, probe failures do not result in an erroneous or ambiguous display. Instead, loss of a CHT probe will simply cause the black bar to disappear from the corresponding cylinder readout, with the EGT display for that cylinder unaffected. Should an EGT probe give out, the entire EGT column for that cylinder will go blank, but the CHT bar—instead of remaining black—will revert to a bright orange bar, telling you that combustion hasn't ceased (rather, just a probe failed). Nor will failure of one probe affect the display for any other.

USING THE GEM ON THE GROUND

The Graphic Engine Monitor is ready to operate as soon as electrical power is applied. Seconds after engine start, as the engine begins putting out hot exhaust gases, orange EGT bars will begin to appear on the GEM display face. (The lowest exhaust gas temperature that can be displayed on the GEM is 800 degrees Fahrenheit. In many engines, the throttle will have to be opened to the "fast idle" range to get an EGT indication for all cylinders.) Within several minutes—as cylinder heads begin to warm up—the CHT display will begin to show CHT for all four or all six cylinders as a dark (non-illuminated) bar in each EGT readout stack. From now until you shut your engine down at the end of the flight, the Graphic Engine Monitor will continue to display CHT and EGT and can be referred to for leaning purposes, or to diagnose possible engine troubles, at any time.

The temperature range of the GEM extends lower than most analog EGT systems to include temperatures normally encountered at startup. (This is possible because the GEM's display scaling is not linear at the lower ranges.) Under normal engine operation at 1,000 to 1,200 rpm a one or two-bar EGT indication will be seen, normally, for each cylinder. The exact indication will vary from one installation to another. It is not unusual to observe fairly large exhaust temperature differences between cylinders at idle or taxi power settings.

Like many other EGT systems, the Graphic Engine Monitor can detect abnormal combustion conditions during the pretakeoff runup. The primary purpose of the pretakeoff engine runup is to verify the integrity of the complete ignition system (from the standpoint not only of magneto timing but also harness, spark plug, and magneto operating condition), and also the functionality of carburetor heat and the propeller control (if present). In the absence of an EGT system that can read accurately at low power settings, pilots are accustomed to detecting engine and/or ignition problems by rpm drop or roughness during the runup. With the GEM, much more accurate diagnosis of problems is possible.

As the engine is run up to 1,700 or 1,800 rpm (or as recommended in your Pilot's Operating Handbook), there will be a rise in EGT for all cylinders, to about one-third of full scale. The "peaks" for the different cylinders will vary somewhat; this is normal. EGT should be carefully observed during the magneto check, since a good deal of information can be gleaned about mag timing and plug condition. Each magneto fires one spark plug in each cylinder, so that during single-mag operation, only one plug is firing in each combustion chamber, and—as a result—with the switch to single-mag operation, an rpm drop of 50 to 150 rpm takes place due to the fact that combustion duration iss longer when there is only one flame front, rather than two. This effectively shifts the point of peak combustion pressure to a later point in the power stroke. The net result is not only a slight loss of rpm, but an *increase* in the indicated EGT. Thus, during single-mag operation on the ground, the exhaust gas temperatures of all cylinders should rise two to four bars.

The *absence* of an rpm drop or EGT rise on single-mag operation indicates trouble in the form of a "hot mag" (broken P-lead) or defective ignition switch (as explained in the chapter on troubleshooting). A more common trouble indication would be the total disappearance of the EGT "bar stack" for one cylinder (occasionally more than one) during the switch to single-mag operation, indicating a faulty ignition wire or spark plug. If the "blanked out" cylinder returns to a normal EGT indication when operating on the other magneto, you have isolated the problem to a particular spark plug (or lead) in a single cylinder—and saved yourself about $40 of shop labor at most

FBOs. Manufacturers' handbooks generally warn pilots to regard any rpm difference of more than 50 rpm between mags as suspicious. It is important to note, however, that the "rpm drop" method is valid only if more plugs are fouling on one mag than on the other. If each magneto harness harbors one bad plug (or lead), the uniformity of the mag drop—when checked by rpm alone—might be such as to be ignored by the average pilot. The double fault could go completely undetected. The Graphic Engine Monitor will leave no doubt as to which cylinder(s) contain bad plugs or leads; a rapid drop in the EGT indication of the affected cylinder(s) gives instantaneous and unambiguous information as to the exact location of the problem. This greatly simplifies the troubleshooting process.

Carburetor heat application causes an extreme reduction in the density (and thus the oxygen content, by volume) of air entering the engine, creating an overrich condition. This can be seen by a large drop in engine rpm, as well as a drop-off of exhaust gas temperature. If carb heat fails to produce these effects, it's likely that the carb heat control is misrigged or the airbox flapper valve is hung open and leaking hot air to the carburetor. This should be remedied as soon as possible, since carb heat on takeoff can reduce detonation margins.

It's a good idea to check the mixture control during runup, too. A uniform rise of EGT indications for all cylinders will confirm the functionality of the mixture control. The exact amount of temperature rise will depend on the degree of mixture control movement, but a GEM EGT rise of four bars or more would be typical before the onset of engine roughness from fuel starvation. Note that each jug should show some rise in EGT upon leaning. Failure of a cylinder to show a rise—or an abnormally large EGT difference between cylinders—could indicate fuel injector nozzle clogging in a fuel-injected engine. In quite a few engines, a large intercylinder EGT spread is normal at low power settings—with or without fuel injection—so a diagnosis of this kind is often impractical until the pilot becomes thoroughly familiar with the normal indications for the engine in question. Still, this type of diagnosis is easily made with the GEM, despite its supposedly "coarse" resolution.

USING THE GEM ON TAKEOFF

Abnormal combustion (preignition and/or detonation) can do extensive damage to an engine in a matter of seconds if left unattended. This type of combustion can be quickly spotted with the GEM.

A quick glance at the GEM will show a dramatic, full-scale (or nearly full-scale) temperature rise in the EGT indication of any cylinder that is undergoing preignition. (Detonation will cause an increase in CHT but a *decrease* in EGT; see Chapter 5.) If an offscale-high indication is noticed during the takeoff roll, the takeoff must be aborted. (If takeoff has already proceeded beyond the point of no return, the throttle setting should be reduced immediately and the mixture enrichened as necessary to cause the temperature to drop in the affected cylinders, and a precautionary landing made as soon as feasible.) Detonation results in poor power output, poor takeoff acceleration, and abnormally low EGT readings (along with, eventually, high CHT readings). The most common cause of detonation on takeoff is misfueling with jet fuel. Mechanical problems can also cause detonation, as can overleaning.

The caveats about detonation notwithstanding, manual leaning during takeoff is advisable for best performance under high-density-altitude conditions (with non-turbocharged engines), and this is something that can be done with accuracy with the GEM. Remember that the full-throttle, full-rich mixture setting is designed to provide an enriched fuel flow for proper engine cooling during takeoff at sea level on a standard day.

The actual magnitude of the overrichness is quite high; it's an FAA-mandated *minimum* of 12 percent more than the worst-case detonation-onset fuel flow (and often as much as 50 percent richer than the best-power fuel flow). With increasing density altitude, this built-in richness gets even worse, taking away more power (ironically) than would normally be lost due to reduced air density alone.

Manual leaning during a high-altitude takeoff can restore a significant amount of power and add significantly to airplane performance. *Consult your Pilot's Operating Handbook for the manufacturer's recommended high-altitude takeoff procedures.* On some factory-installed fuel-flow gauges, the full-power altitude reference markings indicate acceptable fuel flows for various altitudes. In some instances, a specific temperature (e.g., 150 degrees rich of peak EGT) is specified as the takeoff-power mixture setpoint. The Graphic Engine Monitor can be used to set the mixture using this guideline, or (with careful operator technique) to produce the EGT indications typical of a normal sea-level takeoff.

With the GEM 603, TIT can be controlled to precise temperature values, within ten degrees. Four to six bars below the asterisk reference mark (found on the upper left side of the display) is cited by Insight as a typical sea-level takeoff indication.

LEANING THE ENGINE IN FLIGHT

Leaning may be accomplished in climb, cruise, or descent, with the GEM in any mode. The basic cruise-leaning procedure for using the GEM is as follows:

1. Establish cruise altitude. Then establish cruise power. (Make initial trim adjustments, etc., as needed to establish cruise.)

2. Perform a "coarse leaning" or preliminary leaning of the engine. I.e., lean the mixture until the EGT bars rise to a bar or two below the normal cruise indication, or until the fuel flow is within a couple gallons per hour of the anticipated final fuel flow.

3. Pause for two minutes to allow the engine to stabilize in temperature and the turbocharger (if so equipped) to stabilize in output before attempting final leaning. (During this time, you can make final trim adjustments to the airplane, reset cowl flaps, etc.)

4. Push the reset button on the GEM to enter Lean Mode. When you have entered Lean Mode, the EGT annunciator will begin blinking.

5. Now lean the mixture again, slowly, until one of the EGT columns blinks. The flashing stack identifies that cylinder as the leanest, based on the fact that the cylinder in question has just reached or gone slightly past peak EGT, in advance of any other cylinder. Push the reset button briefly to stop the blinking. (The instrument will now be in Monitor Mode.)

6. Enrichen the mixture as desired. (Push reset button again to "store" existing exhaust gas temperatures for Monitor Mode.)

These are the basics of leaning with the Graphic Engine Monitor. Because of the many differences between engines with respect to fuel metering, horsepower output, cylinder and valve construction, turbo-charging, etc., no one set of leaning recommendations will be right for all owners.

The choice of a leaning procedure for a particular aircraft engine should be based on a thorough understanding of combustion dynamics and mission variables (see Chapters Two and Three), as with any EGT system. It is highly advisable, however, for owners of turbo-charged aircraft to take advantage of the extra display capabilities of the GEM 603, which adds a numeric TIT readout to the top of the cockpit display. Turbocharged engine operators who install the GEM 602 (which does not have TIT capability) are doing their engines a disservice. No TIO- or TSIO-series engine should be without a calibrated TIT readout on the panel.

Insight Instrument Corporation's own *Pilot's Guide* to the GEM contains much additional useful information on the operation of the Graphic Engine Monitor (and interpretation of EGT data in general). For a copy of the *Pilot's Guide,* write or call Insight at Box 194, Ellicott Station, Buffalo, NY 14205 (phone 416/871-0733).

Glossary

A/F ratio: air-to-fuel ratio, by mass.

aftercooler: see *intercooler.*

alcohol: Generic term for compounds of the form X-O-H, where X is a hydrocarbon group (methyl, ethyl, propyl, butyl, or whatever).

ambient: local surrounding (as in "ambient air temperature," which is the temperature of the air surrounding the airplane).

angle-valve engine: Any cylinder head in which the intake and exhaust valves are not parallel. Angle-valve heads have better knock resistance and volumetric efficiency than parallel-valve heads. Parallel-valve heads have the principal advantage of being cheaper to produce.

aromatic: A generic term for a class of hydrocarbons molecules based on a double-bonded six-carbon cyclic (ring structure) backbone. The simplest aromatic hydrocarbon is benzene, formula C_6H_6. Toluene, xylene, and other aromatics are often found in gasoline (avgas as well as mogas). They are used as blending agents to give good antiknock performance (high octane rating).

ATC: After top center (of piston travel)

austenitic: Carbon-containing iron alloy.

autoignition: Self-ignition (as of a fuel-air mixture). Ignition without spark initiation.

barrel: The portion of the cylinder in which the piston travels back and forth (as opposed to the head portion, which contains the valves).

BBC: Before bottom center.

best-economy mixture: The mixture setting or fuel/air ratio producing the optimum specific fuel consumption, generally found at an EGT around 50 degrees (F) on the lean side of peak.

best-power mixture: The mixture setting or fuel/air ratio producing the most power from a given amount of airflow into the engine. This mixture is generally found at an EGT around 125 degrees (F) on the rich side of peak.

bhp: Brake horsepower—the actual amount of horsepower delivered from an engine's crankshaft to a test-stand brake.

BMEP: Brake mean effective pressure. A measure of the average pressure (in psi) developed within a cylinder, based on actual brake horsepower, rpm, and displacement. BMEP is directly proportional to power output, and inversely proportional to displacement and rpm.

boost: Extra manifold pressure resulting from turbocharger or super-charger output.

boost pump: Auxiliary electric fuel pump.

bootstrapping: An unstable manifold pressure condition which can occur in turbocharged aircraft in high-altitude cruise with the waste-gate closed, wherein large, unexpected manifold-pressure excursions take place spontaneously. The instability is due to feedback-loop effects in the turbo system.

Bourdon tube: A miniature inflatable, coiled tube which is often used in oil pressure and other types of instruments to drive a meter movement.

brake mean effective pressure: See *BMEP* above.

BTC: Before top center (of piston travel).

BTU: British Thermal Unit. The amount of energy needed to raise the temperature of a pound of water one degree Fahrenheit.

camshaft: A shaft with metal lobes on it to trip open the engine's intake and exhaust valves at the right time and in the right order. The camshaft determines valve opening times and durations relative to the Otto cycle.

charge: Fuel-air charge—the incoming mix of fuel and air as it arrives at the combustion chamber.

CHT: Cylinder head temperature. The temperature of the large, finned end of the cylinder containing the valves.

compression ratio: The ratio of the combustion-chamber volume with the piston at the bottom limit of its travel to the combustion-chamber volume with the piston at the *top* limit of its travel. Values of 6.5:1 to 9:1 are common in aircraft engines. High compression ratios permit efficient power production but require the use of higher-octane gasolines.

crankshaft: The main power-transmitting shaft of the engine.

creep: The tendency of a metal to become plastic and flow at high temperatures.

critical altitude: In a turbocharged aircraft, the altitude above which sea-level rated manifold pressure can no longer be maintained; or the altitude above which the wastegate is closed all the way, all the time.

cylinder: The mechanical assembly in which combustion takes place, consisting of a barrel and a head, with rocker-actuated poppet valves contained in the head portion.

cylinder head temperature (CHT): The temperature of the head portion of the cylinder, as measured by a thermocouple placed either in the spark plug area or a threaded boss in the head.

detonation: Combustion knock—the premature, spontaneous auto-ignition of the unburned fuel-air charge ahead of the flame front, in a combustion chamber in which discharge of the spark plug(s) has already occurred. Detonation can be caused by fuel of insufficient octane rating, or (with the proper octane fuel) operation a too high a power output with too lean a mixture. Improperly advanced magneto itiming will also encourage detonation, as will heating of the incoming fuel-air charge (by carburetor heat or by compression via turbo-charger). Compare *preignition*.

diesel: A class of piston engine in which compression of the fuel is (by itself) used for ignition, in lieu of spark ignition.

displacement: The cylinder cross-section area multiplied by the piston travel (stroke), multiplied by the number of pistons in the engine.

EGT: Exhaust gas temperature.

exhaust port: The area of the cylinder head immediately outside the combustion chamber on the exhaust-valve side.

expansion cycle: The power stroke in a four-stroke-cycle engine.

F/A ratio: Fuel-to-air ratio, by mass.

four-stroke cycle: Also called *Otto cycle.* This is the familiar power production cycle in which fuel and air are drawn into the cylinder on the piston downstroke; the fuel/air charge is compressed on the next piston upstroke; combustion takes place on the subsequent downstroke; and exhaust gases are expelled from the combustion chamber on the following upstroke. All current production aircraft engines are of the reciprocating (vs. rotary/Wankel), spark-ignition (vs. diesel), four-stroke-cycle (vs. two-stroke cycle) type.

FWF: Firewall-forward.

GEM: Graphic Engine Monitor (by Insight Instrument Corporation).

heptane: A 7-carbon-long hydrocarbon. Normal heptane (straight-chain heptane) has conspicuously poor antiknock properties and is used as the zero reference in Graham Edgar's octane scale.

hydrocarbon: Generic term for compounds consisting solely of hydrogen and carbon atoms.

IAS: Indicated airspeed, as measured by a pitot-static type airspeed indicator system.

Inconel: Trade name for a family of high-nickel superalloys resistant to corrosion at high temperatures.

induction system: Broadly, the entire air-intake system of the engine, from airscoop to intake ports.

intake manifold: The system of piping by which air is delivered to the cylinders.

intake port: The area of the cylinder head immediately outside the combustion chamber on the intake-valve side.

intercooler: A radiator placed in the induction system of a turbo-charged engine, between the turbo compressor outlet and the throttle butterfly. The purpose of the intercooler is to cool the intake air.

J-type thermocouple: An iron/constantan thermocouple (designed for use at temperatures to 1,200 degrees Fahrenheit).

knock: see *Detonation*.

K-type thermocouple: A chromel/alumel thermocouple (designed for operation at temperatures up to 2,000 degrees Fahrenheit).

lean misfire: Stumbling or roughness due to inadequate fuel in the fuel/air mixture.

leanest cylinder: The cylinder that operates at the lowest overall fuel/air ratio compared to the other cylinders in the engine. By the EGT method, leanest cylinder is defined as the cylinder that reaches peak-EGT first during progressive leanout.

manifold pressure: The pressure, in inches of mercury, of air within the engine induction system downstream of the throttle butterfly. This pressure is directly related to air flow and hence (under most circumstances) engine power output.

MP: Manifold pressure.

Nimonic: Trade name for a family of nickel alloys made for high-temperature applications. Nimonic 80A and 90 are widely used in Continental and Lycoming exhaust valves.

Ni-resist: A heat- and corrosion-resistant nickel-iron alloy.

Nitralloy: Proprietary name for a particular nitride-hardened steel alloy used by Teledyne Continental in some (but not all) valve guides.

nitriding: A surface-hardening procedure applicable to certain steel alloys, which gives extra durability in applications where metal-to-metal sliding contact occurs.

normally aspirated: Refers to any engine that does not employ super-charging or turbocharging.

normalize: Restore manifold pressure to sea-level equivalency via turbocharging.

NTSB: National Transportation Safety Board.

octane: The name of a C8 hydrocarbon. With reference to detonation, octane refers to gasoline antiknock performance as rated by Graham Edgar's octane scale. In the octane scale, knock performance equates to the percentage (by volume) of iso-octane that must be added to n-heptane to give a reference fuel that exactly mimics the knock intensity of a sample fuel.

Otto cycle: see *four-stroke-cycle* above.

OAT: Outside air temperature. The temperature of the atmosphere outside the airplane.

overboost: Any condition which causes an engine to operate in excess of maximum design horsepower. In a turbocharged engine, it refers to operation beyond redline manifold pressure.

P-lead: Magneto breaker point lead wire.

piston: The reciprocating (back-and-forth-moving) metal part that transfers pressure from combustion to the crankshaft.

piston rings: Large, thin, C-shaped pieces of metal (cast iron, generally) that ride in grooves in the side of the piston and the function of which is to seal the combustion chamber gas-tight for efficient combustion.

PMA: Parts Manufacturer Approval. A type of manufacturing approval granted by FAA.
poppet valve: A tulip-shaped valve (see *valve*).

preignition: Initiation of combustion in a cylinder before the normal discharge of the spark plug. Anything that causes premature initiation of combustion can be said to be causing preignition. Because of the abnormal stresses and temperatures induced, preignition can be extremely damaging to an engine, often resulting in piston holing/ melting. Preignition causes very high CHT indications.

pressure ratio: In turbocharging, the ratio of outlet to inlet pressure at the turbo compressor.

psi: Pounds per square inch. A measure of pressure. (One psi is approximately equal to two inches of mercury.)

radical: Molecular fragment with one valence (bond) unsatisfied. For example, hydrogen peroxide, formula H-O-O-H, can cleave in half to form two hydroxyl (OH) radicals. Radicals are extremely reactive and almost certainly play a key role in normal and abnormal combustion propagation.

ram rise: Rise in air pressure due to ram effect of high-speed air on a scoop or orifice.

Rankine: A temperature scale starting at absolute zero, but using Fahrenheit-type degree divisions. (The equivalent scale using Celsius-type degrees is called the Kelvin scale.) Absolute zero, or zero degrees Rankine, occurs at minus 460 Fahrenheit.

SAE: Society of Automotive Engineers.

sfc: Specific fuel consumption, usually given in pounds of fuel per hour per horsepower (lbs/bhp/hr).

SFRM: Time (in hours) since factory remanufacture of the engine.

SMOH: Time (in hours) since major overhaul.

STOH: Time (in hours) since top overhaul.

stoichiometric: Refers to the mass-balance conditions in which every reactant in a chemical reaction has the potential of being used up completely, with no reactants left over. A stoichiometric fuel-air mixture is one in which the ratio of oxygen to fuel is perfectly balanced so that neither is present in excess.

supercharger: Any device that forcibly increases the amount of air flowed by an engine's induction system. A turbocharger is a type of supercharger.

TBO: Time between overhauls.

TCP: Tricresyl phosphate, a lead-scavenging gasoline additive.

TEL: Tetraethyl lead, a potent antiknock additive.

thermocouple: A junction between two dissimilar metal alloys in which a small voltage is produced which varies with temperature. The voltage is produced because different metals have different tendencies to "donate" their electrons. At the microscopic level, the individual grains of metal can be thought of as surrounded by an electron cloud or vapor, which has a "vapor pressure" characteristic of the particular metal. With increasing temperature, the "pressure" of the electron cloud increases. This pressure is responsible for the voltage difference at the thermocouple junction. Different alloys are used in thermocouples for different heat range applications; for example, EGT probes use chromel and alumel, while thermocouples in the 300 to 600 degree Fahrenheit range often use copper and constantan, others use iron and constantan, etc.

TIT: Turbine inlet temperature. The average temperature of the exhaust entering the turbine portion of a turbocharger.

turbocharger: An exhaust-driven supercharger (see "supercharger" above), used for increasing the manifold pressur and total power output of an engine.

valve: Tulip-shaped valves are used to admit fuel and air into the aircraft engine cylinder, and also to let exhaust gases out. (Valves thus fall into two categories: intake and exhaust.) The valves are normally kept closed by spring pressure. They open in response to rocker and pushrod action, which in turn depends on the pushing action of lobes on a camshaft. The camshaft (see "camshaft" above) is in turn gear-driven by the crankshaft, at half crankshaft speed. Intake valves normally operate at a much lower temperature than exhaust valves, due to the cooling afforded by incoming fuel and air. Exhaust valves often employ special alloys and construction techniques. Exhaust valves are very sensitive to mixture leaning and EGT; when EGT is high, exhaust valve temperature is high. (Sometimes even when EGT is low, exhaust valve temperature is high.) Proper valve operation is essential to optimum engine performance. Both intake and exhaust valves spend approximately two-thirds of their time shut, in normal operation.

valve guide: A cylindrical piece of metal, about three inches in length, in which the valve stem (of either an intake or exhaust valve) slides back and forth. Valve guides for aircraft engines may be made of aluminum-bronze, cast iron, or nitrided steel. They are a hot part of an aircraft engine and are sensitive to operator technique where leaning is concerned.

volumetric efficiency: The ratio of the *actual* amount of air passed through a cylinder (or an engine) in one complete Otto cycle to the cylinder's (or engine's) *displacement*. Volumetric efficiency is an indirect measure of combustion efficiency. For a normally aspirated aircraft engine, a V.E. of 70-80% is typical. Volumetric efficiencies of well over 100 percent are possible with turbocharging/supercharging.

wastegate: A control valve (which may be of either the butterfly or poppet type) in the exhaust system which governs the flow of exhaust to a turbocharger turbine. Closing the wastegate increases the flow through the turbocharger. Wastegates may be manually controllable or automatically actuated.

Index

Abnormal combustion ....81 ff
Adapter probe..125
Alcohol in fuel 111
Annunciation 135
Antiknock performance (see Octane, Detonation, etc.)
Ash deposits..108
ASTM D-439 (auto fuel specficiation) 112
ASTM D-910 37
Auto fuel 93, 113
Avgas 100LL..60
Best-economy, cylinder life and 71
Best-power mixture..40, 61
Boeing Stratocruiser 2
Brake mean effective pressure (BMEP) 95
BTU content of fuels 36-37
Cam lobe profile 29
Carb heat
    detonation and 96
    EGT spread and 46
Carbon deposits on valves 77
Carbon monoxide 41
Cessna Aircraft
    177B leaning procedure 2
    182 45
    402 50
    Skymaster..105
    T210...30
    Turbo 310 ....73, (photo) 74
CHT (cylinder head temperature)
    adapter probe, Insight 125
    annunciation 75
    detonation and 79
    GEM display of 69
    leaning by reference to 2
    preignition and 108

CHT (cylinder head temperature), continued
    redlines 11
    troubleshooting with .... 78 ff, 103
    vs. EGT 38
Clearance volume 25
Cobalt alloy drill bits 117
Cold junction 119
Combustion 34
    peak temperatures during 41
    unstable 44-45
Compensation circuitry 119
Compression ratio 25
    best-economy mixture and 65
    detonation and 83
Compression stroke .... 14 ff, 25 ff
Continental (see Teledyne)
Continuous-flow injection 23
Cooling
    effect of valve timing on 18
    fuel 10
    oil 10
    vs. ignition timing 20
Cowl flaps 11
Creep 60
    iron alloys and 48
Cruise leaning .... 59 ff
Cylinder
    construction (diagram) 19
    cooldown rate, acceptable 71
    fuel cooling 10
    hottest 47
    leanest, finding 40, 47
    overheating .... 75 ff
    parallel-valve 19
Cylinder compression 106-107
Deck air temperature 53
Delco (Dayton Engineering Laboratories) 83
Density altitude, leaning and 34
Descent, leaning in 71

Detonation 11, 107
    compression ratio and 27
    CHT and 79
    early research on ....86 ff
    in TIO-540 (photo) 81
    in TIO-540-J2BD (graph) 52
    mode of action of...90 ff
    margin of protection, FAA-required 55
    trace 93
    turbocharged engines and 53
Diesel, Rudolf...18
Differential compression test 28
Digital vs analog display..132
Displacement 25
Drill bits 116
Dynacam engine 14
Edgar, Graham...84
EGT (exhaust gas temperature)
    alcohols and 112
    cycle-by-cycle variations in 6
    detonation and...94 ff
    digital vs. analog 132
    fuel-air ratio ....38 ff
    graph of theoretical vs. actual...5
    peak...6
    spread, intercylinder ....44 ff
    vs. fuel-air ratio ....6 ff
EGT spread 66
Electronics International 132
Enstrom helicopter 116
Ergonomics ....129 ff
Ethyl Corporation 84
Exhaust analyzer 3
Flame propagation 19
Fuel contamination 110
Fuel flow, EGT vs. 38,42
Fuel injection 23
Fuel maldistribution 23
Fuel-air ratio, EGT and ....38 ff
Fuel-flow gauge, leaning by 57

Gasoline 36
   alcohol-contaminated 112
   high-octane 89
GEM (see Insight)
Gibson, Prof. A.H. 82
Ground leaning 147
Guides, valve 49
Harness, EGT probe 117
Heat content of fuels 113
Heywood, John B. 45
Hot junction 119
Hottest cylinder (vs. leanest) 4
Howard, Dee 2
Hundere, Al 1
Hydraulic lifters 109
Hydrocarbons, chemistry of 84
Ideal T-stripper 120
Idle, leaning at 57
Ignition timing (see Timing)
Inconel 60
Induction air leaks 106
Injector nozzles 23, 106
   obstruction of 24
Insight GEM 47
   CHT adaptor 125
   description of 139
   installation of 116
   Model 603 150
   Monitor Mode 104
   operation of ....Appendix B
Insight Instrument Corporation 9
Intake valves 14, 48
Intercooling 30
Intercylinder EGT spread 66
Iso-octane, structure of 85
Isomers 85
J-type thermocouple 125
J.P. Instruments 75
Jet fuel 110
Johnson, Ken 70

Kerosene 83
Kettering, Charles...83
Knock (see Detonation)
KS Avionics ....(photo) 102, 137 ff
   Hexad II...134
Lag, probe 9
LCD (liquid crystal display) gauges 129
Lead (see Tetraethyl lead)
Lean misfire..44
Lean-burn engine design..96, 97
Leanest cylinder ....40 ff
Liquid-cooled engines 97
Lycoming (see Textron)
Magneto failure, EGT and 103
Magnetos, pressurized 30
Maldistribution, fuel ....43 ff
Manifold pressure defined..22
Methyl alcohol (methanol) 37
Midgely, Thomas...86
Misfire, lean..44
Mixture
   best-economy ....41, 64 ff
   best-power...40 ff, 61
   changes with altitude ....34 ff
   peak-EGT ....63 ff
Mixture schedule, designed-in 55
Mooney 231 30
Multichannel EGTs ....130 ff
Multiprobe systems ....129 ff
N-heptane, structure of 85
Nimonic alloy 60
Nitralloy valve guides 49
Octane anomalies 88
Octane rating system..85 ff
   rich vs. lean method...87 ff
Oil, cooling effect of 10
Oil consumption, excessive...107
Oils, ash-forming 108
Otto cycle ....14 ff
Overheating ....75 ff

Overheating, cylinder .... 69 ff
Overtemp annunciation 137
Panel, instrument 122
Peak-EGT limitations 50, 63ff
Pencil lead 116
Performance Numbers 88
Peroxides 111
Piper Aircraft
  Aerostar 601 61
  Lance 140
  Malibu 43
  Pressurized Navajo 26
  Seminole 137
  Turbo Lance 30
Piston failure 92, 107
Power stroke 15
Preignition 107
  vs. detonation 27
  due to jet fuel 110
  runaway 92
Probe lag 9, 47
Probe siting .... 75, 115 ff
Probes
  physics of .... 99 ff
  TIT, installing 119
Probes, EGT 6-7
  response time 9
Pull test 121
Radicals 35
Rajay turbos 52
Range (aircraft), leaning and 43
Readability, EGT display 132
Red wire, thermocouple 117
Redline (see CHT, TIT, etc.)
Resolution 142
Resolution, display 7
Ricardo, Harry 82
Rolls-Royce Merlin 87
Runaway preignition 92
Runup leaning 148

Scanning EGTs 130
Shock cooling .... 69 ff
Single-mag operation 103
Soapstone 120
Sodium-filled valves .... 48 ff
Spark plug fouling .... 104 ff
Specific fuel consumption 20
    leaning for best 42
    stoichiometry vs. 65
    vs. EGT 38
Stoichiometry .... 36 ff
Stratified charge engine 96
Stripper, wire 120
Superalloys 48
Supercharging 29
Swearingen, Ed 1
Switchable EGTs .... 130 ff
Takeoff leaning 56-57, 149
Tappets 17, 109
Taylor, C.F. 60
TBO (Time Between Overhauls) 60, 67, 75
Teledyne Continental
    C-75 65
    C-series 64
    GTSIO-520 51
    IO-520-B 24
    IO-520 mixture schedule .... 55 ff
    IO-520 series 25-27
    IOL- & TIOL-series 97
    leaning recommendations 49
    O-470-R 45-46, 63
    TSIO-520-BE 43, 67
Tetraethyl lead (TEL) .... 86 ff
Textron Lycoming
    Flyer article 70
    HIO-360 116
    IGSO-series 64
    IO-540-A 24
    leaning recommendations 49
    O-235-L 63, 67

Textron Lycoming, continued
O-320-E2D 61
O-360-E 65
O-320-H & O-360-E 109
O-360 Operator's Handbook advice 75
Service Instruction 1094C 6
TIGO-series 64
TIO-540-J2BD, detonation in 54
TIO-541 series 63
Thermocouples
chromel-alumel 7
CHT 10
installation .... 115 ff
physics of .... 99 ff
Type J 9
Type K 9
Timing
ignition, and detonation .... 91 ff
spark 18
spark, and cylinder cooling 20-21
spark, and turbocharged engines 29
spark, sfc and 20
valve 16-17
valve and spark, effect on EGT .... 101 ff
TIT (turbine inlet temp) .... 50 ff
limits 52
TOT (Turbine outlet temperature) 1
Troubleshooting, EGT and .... 99 ff
Tuning, induction 24, 44,45
Turbocharger
schematic of TH08A 26
ni-resist housings 52
Turbocharging .... 28 ff
Two-stroke-cycle engines 15
Upgrading .... 129 ff
Valve lash 17
Valve lead/lag 15
Valve overlap 15
Valve seats 70
Valve sticking .... 70 ff

Valve, exhaust 15
   rotation of 77
   size of vs. intake 29
   sodium-filled 48
Volatility, fuel 113
Wastegate 30